TART

AND

SWEET

TART
AND
SWEET

101
CANNING AND
PICKLING RECIPES
FOR THE
MODERN KITCHEN

KELLY GEARY AND JESSIE KNADLER

RODALE

Rodale books may be purchased for business or promotional use or for special sales. For information,
please write to: Special Markets Department, Rodale Inc., 733 Third Avenue, New York, NY 10017.

Printed in the United States of America
Rodale Inc. makes every effort to use acid-free ♾, recycled paper ♻.

Book design by Kara Plikaitis
Photographs by Ellen Silverman

Library of Congress Cataloging-in-Publication Data

Geary, Kelly.
    Tart and sweet : 101 canning and pickling recipes for the modern kitchen / Kelly Geary and Jessie Knadler.
        p.   cm.
    Includes bibliographical references and index.
    ISBN 978–1–60529–382–0 hardcover
    1. Canning and preserving.   2. Vegetables—Preservation.   3. Fruit—Preservation.   I. Knadler, Jessie.   II. Title.   III. Title:
Tart and sweet.
    TX603.G43 2010
    664'.0282—dc22   2010030226

Distributed to the trade by Macmillan
2   4   6   8   10   9   7   5   3   1   hardcover

RODALE

We inspire and enable people to improve their lives and the world around them.
www.rodalebooks.com

Jessie

Kelly

TO Our Families

HOME MADE
BRAND
PRESERVES
MANUFACTURED BY
A. JOHNSON CO.
BOSTON
CANNING

Contents

Canning Basics

Recipes

Ideas and Solutions

Introduction

I'm always thrilled and amazed by the number of people who show up each night for the canning workshops I offer in my Sweet Deliverance kitchen. Curious home cooks, foodies, and back to basics–minded men and women alike hover around my worktable—sometimes it's standing room only—as I explain the fundamentals of pickling and jamming, interrupted by the occasional *ping!* of jars cooling on a nearby shelf. (My shelves are so loaded with canned goods, in fact, that you might mistake me for a pioneer woman if my business weren't located on the second floor on a busy Brooklyn street.) I get asked a lot of questions—two of the most common being "How long does canned food last?" (answer: Officially, a year; unofficially, a long, long time) and "Is sugar what preserves the food?" (answer: No, but more about that later). For me, the crowd and their curiosity are evidence of just how popular home preserving has become. There's the rustic appeal of wanting to know where your food comes from and the allure of saving the seasonal bounty for later, for sure, but I think this canning resurgence taps into something deeper: People want to know how to make things with their hands that are more tangible, more meaningful than sliding a mouse across a pad or queuing up a playlist on an iPod. "Putting up" (that's preserving lingo for canning and jarring) even a small amount of food is a reminder that we *can* take care of ourselves, feed ourselves and our families, without always relying on food manufacturers to do it for us. Canning is self-sufficiency in a jar.

I think it's because of this innate desire for a life that is made, not bought, that home canned goods make such wonderful gifts. Once I discovered that my friends, family members, and clients seemed to appreciate a quart of pickled asparagus or a pint of banana rum butter so much more than a store-bought trinket, I all but stopped shopping for gifts and started making them.

But not all benefits of canning are so high-minded: With a bunch of canned food lying around, I'm never at a loss for what to feed friends who happen to stop by. A few pickles, a bit of cheese, some fruit spreads, and bread on a plate make a fast, easy, and delicious snack. And cocktails! I use my canned creations to concoct the tastiest drinks—like mixing candied kumquats and Prosecco to serve up my famous (some might say infamous) Kumma Closer (see page 197 for the recipe).

And although canning involves an initial investment of time and labor, it makes for faster cooking down the line. I live in a cozy one-bedroom Brooklyn apartment, and I put up food (not a lot, since my home kitchen is pretty small) to make subsequent meals—spaghetti with canned tomatoes with sardines and Pecorino, apple butter for baking, carrot daikon pickles for my beloved Banh Mi—so I don't have to spend a lot of time cooking during my off-hours. In these pages, you'll find plenty of recipes—from salads and main courses to desserts and cocktails—that incorporate your home canned goods with delicious results.

When I was growing up in Naples, Florida, no one around me canned. It's not something I learned by watching my mother or grandmother sweat over a hot cauldron. As a kid, I never even went *camping*, let alone *canning*. Like a lot of Americans at that time, I was about as out of touch with where my food actually came from as a person could be. It wasn't until I moved to Northern California at the age of 23 and got a job working on the crepe truck at a farmers' market that I realized how much I loved working with food, and being around people who shared that passion. This market, in a town called Arcata, was *the* place to socialize on the weekends—everybody (and their dog) came to hang out. There was always a band jamming in the background. Local farmers' booths were stacked high with teacup-size morel mushrooms and wild asparagus so fresh and juicy it could be eaten raw. It was a far cry from the tomatoes and strawberries and tropical produce I was used to; there were things like kale and winter squash, mushrooms you could pick yourself, and seaweed you could harvest. I made friends with farmers and growers, most of whom were my age. I'd never met a farmer under the age of 30—I didn't even know it was a viable career option for someone my age (how wrong I was)! Being around these people, and learning from them, made me realize that I needed to work with *real* food. Not the stuff that's shipped across the country on a Sysco truck.

So I hit the road for New York City, where I became a student at the Natural Gourmet Institute. There, I learned about the health benefits of preserved food and that the typical American diet—unlike other world cuisines with a rich preserving heritage (Middle Eastern, Asian, Mediterranean)—is lacking in bitter and sour flavors. I began poring through canning cookbooks, new and old, and preserving things like kimchi and other fermented vegetables, which led to a serious interest in all things canned. Pretty soon I was swapping recipes with equally canning-mad friends and asking questions about how to make preserved foods healthier. Namely, why is there so much sugar in the average jam recipe? Are 5 cups of sugar really necessary to make something as simple as apple butter? To learn more about canning science, I enrolled in the Better Process Control School at Cornell University and realized that most of the sugar called for in canning recipes is more about satisfying America's sweet tooth than about actually preserving the food.

But over the past few decades, our palates have started to change and evolve. So I started carefully developing my own recipes that reflect how people like me and my friends like to eat today. I began tinkering with different flavor pairings—blueberry lemongrass syrup, ramp kimchi, pickled nettles; interesting combinations I thought would pique the interest of friends who were also part of the booming Brooklyn food scene.

Soon enough, canning went from being a fun, creative hobby to part of my job as a chef. My company, Sweet Deliverance—a food delivery service that makes fresh, ready-to-eat meals from local farm CSA shares—was really starting to take off. But as with any community-supported agriculture (CSA) program, each week's offering is a reflection of the farmer's seasonal bounty. In the fall, for example, I had crates and crates of apples to work with. But my clients could eat only so many of my homemade apple pies, apple crumbles, and apple galettes each week. So I canned the extra apples and gave them as gifts to clients at the end of the season. The delight they found in these homemade goods made me realize there was a cookbook waiting to be written—one that tapped into people's desire for this old-timey craft, but upgraded to reflect the way we live and eat today. So I teamed up with writer Jessie Knadler—who started canning after moving from Manhattan to rural Virginia a few years ago—to bring our passion for preserving to you.

If you're holding this book right now, there's a good chance you too have recently awakened to the idea of home preserving. Maybe you want to start putting up your own fruits and vegetables as a way to trim your weekly grocery bills. Maybe you've recently planted your first garden and are shocked (as Jessie was) by how many cucumbers just one plant can kick out. Maybe you crave to eat closer to the source. Perhaps you're a wee bit alarmed by the recent spate of food scares (salmonella, *E. coli*) that have resulted from our industrial food supply. Or maybe you think canning is a funky craft that could be a fun way to show off your culinary chops (and make great presents that will impress your friends). In all likelihood, it's a combination of all the above. We wrote this book for you.

Our goal is to explain the art and science of home preserving in a straightforward, easy-to-follow manner. The recipes are organized seasonally not only to coincide with nature's harvest when flavors are at their peak—citrus in winter, asparagus in spring, tomatoes in summer, pears in autumn—but as a reflection of the growing desire to eat in a more natural way. We offer recipes for more adventurous types who think outside the Ball jar—horseradish lemon pepper sunchokes, anyone? Pickled endive?—as well as traditional, crowd-pleasing favorites like dilly beans and raspberry jam. We've also made canning healthier by cutting down on the crazy amounts of sugar that are common in older recipes.

Another issue we address: the time factor. Chances are, you're not interested in preserving an entire strawberry patch, just the 3 pounds or so you picked up at your local farm stand. So we scaled the yields with canners like you in mind—people who may have limited time and canning space. But some yields, such as canned tomatoes, we left on the larger end of the spectrum, because it's no fun running out of such cooking staples in the doldrums of February.

This is not an exhaustive manual—we've reviewed and condensed the overwhelming amount of canning information out there so you can focus on having a good time while preserving, and not feel like you're studying for a food science exam. After all, canning is fun! So think of this book as Canning 101. We'll focus on the simplest, easiest canning technique there is, water bath canning, which is used to preserve high-acid foods such as tomatoes, pickles, fruit, and fruit spreads.

Once you've mastered your skills and discovered a few recipes you can't live without, throw a canning party! After all, home preserving is a craft that's meant to be shared . . . more hands in the kitchen make for easier, speedier work. In Chapter 9, we'll show you how to throw a killer canning party. And once you've put up several pints of blueberries or pearl onions—why not share the love? Also in that chapter, we'll show you simple, creative ways to gussy up your jars to make perfect presents.

We hope that with this book you'll wonder how you ever got along *not* canning. Because there's something so supremely gratifying about opening a jar of your own homemade chutney to serve at a dinner party in the dead of winter or giving away jars of apple maple butter as gifts.

We should know—whenever we detect a hint of canning envy from one of our cooking-mad friends (and yes, such a thing exists), we do what any good canner would do: We give them a jar of our DIY creations. Because one thing we know firsthand—there's a whole lot of love that goes into each and every jar.

—Kelly Geary

CANNING
BASICS

Canning *Isn't* Rocket Science

One of the most common misconceptions about canning is that it's hard.

The craft still conjures up images of a 1930s-era housewife shucking a mountain of corn at her kitchen table while a pressure canner rattles and hisses nearby like a bomb about to explode. And for many years, this was a fairly accurate portrait. Before the advent of the processed food industry, people had to preserve food—lots of it—if they wanted to eat fruits and vegetables in February. In fact, we came across a home canning guide from 1935 that called for putting up *560 quarts* of fruits and vegetables for a family of five *every year*. No wonder canning went the way of the carpet beater for so long.

Today, of course, people no longer have to preserve seasonal produce. They choose to do it because it's a delicious, homemade way to eat just a little bit closer to the land, whether you're making pickles from green market cucumbers or tomato sauce from your backyard bounty.

Yet anymore, it seems there's an excessively cautious *If you're not careful, canning may kill you* tone that surrounds the craft. One friend balked before digging into Jessie's homemade peach butter, "Wait, does this have botulism? Is it going to kill me?" Maybe it's because preserving has undergone a resurgence only within the past few years, so it still seems "new" to many, thus scarier than it actually is. Improvements in culinary science and revamped rules and regulations from the US Department of Agriculture have made canning safer than ever, but the flip side is that it now *seems* more nerve-racking than ever. Headspace, processing times, pH levels, altitude considerations—perusing a modern canning manual can feel like studying for a chemistry exam.

The truth: Canning couldn't be simpler, especially the kind we deal with here—*water bath* canning. In fact, very little has changed about canning since it was first invented by a French chef and confectioner (not a scientist, notably) more than 200 years ago. Which is to say, if you can boil water and chop produce, you can *can* like the best of them. Heck, committing to a 48-hour training program (the equivalent of 2 days) is all that's required to call yourself a Master Preserver.

Another fact: Canning won't kill you. We'll get more into the science later, but rest assured, the scary botulism spores you may have read about cannot grow in high-acid food. And the instructions and recipes in this book are written

How Nutritious Is Canned Food?

A lot of people think canned food isn't nearly as nutritious as fresh, and for the most part, that's true—assuming the "fresh" stuff wasn't picked well before peak ripeness or shipped halfway around the world, lingering for days, even weeks in storage, which is often the case for the fruits and vegetables you'll find at your local grocery store.

The reason canned food is sometimes (and erroneously) thought of as a nutritional black hole is because food scientists have generally looked to vitamin C—which happens to be extrasensitive to heat, light, and oxygen—as a measure of nutrient degradation. And it's true, vitamin C, along with equally sensitive B vitamins, degrades rapidly during canning. But they degrade just as rapidly during cooking. In fact, they degrade rapidly just after harvest. Studies have found that vitamin C loss during canning ranged from 10 to 90 percent. Losses during cooking ranged from 15 to 55 percent, while losses during refrigeration for 7 days ranged from 15 to 77 percent. Vitamin C just doesn't like to stick around for very long.

But fruits and vegetables are more than repositories for vitamin C and B vitamins. Studies have shown that fat-soluble nutrients such as vitamins A and E remain more or less constant during heat processing (and levels of disease-preventing carotenoids such as lycopene actually increase). Fiber, minerals, calcium, and potassium remain stable as well.

So to get the most nutritional bang for your preserving buck, try to can local, perfectly ripe, organic fruits and vegetables as soon as possible after harvest to preserve these valuable nutrients. During processing, remaining vitamin C and B vitamins, which are water soluble, may leach into the canning liquid, which can be added to other recipes and consumed.

All that aside, a lot of home canned food falls into the condiment/snack category (dilly beans, fruit spreads, salsas) anyway, which most people don't eat for nutritional purposes. They eat preserved goodies because they taste good and the ingredients are of the highest quality (close to home!), and making jams and pickles is rewarding and fun.

for high-acid canning—fruits, fruit spreads, acidified tomatoes, pickled products, relishes, chutneys, ketchup—products most modern canners are eager to preserve.

So . . . canning is easy. It's safe. You could even call it *modern*. We don't feel that canning is a throwback to another era, an attempt to recapture the halcyon days of Grandma's dilly beans or a romantic nod to a more rustic way of life when smocks and sunbonnets were at the height of fashion. Instead, we believe canning's resurgence can be attributed to the natural outgrowth of the locavore movement. Canning *is* an extension of the way people think about food and the environment today, whether you live in the city, like Kelly, or in the country, like Jessie.

That said, like all DIY hobbies, canning is not without its minor challenges. We've compiled a list of our top seven canning rules—guidelines that will keep the craft fun, easy, and delicious, whether you're a new or longtime preserver.

1. THINK PINTS, NOT PECKS

There's no getting around it: Canning requires food prep—chopping, coring, seeding, and slicing. If you come across a recipe that calls for pounds of fruits and vegetables in multiples of 10 (you'll find only one in this book), you may want to step away from the stove top or call some friends for reinforcement (see rule 7). You'll be spending a long time in the kitchen, veering into "'30s housewife chore" territory.

Kelly speaks from experience on this one. How about the day she thought she'd have a swell time making strawberry jam from four cases of strawberries? By midafternoon she was sweating profusely, her fingertips were stained pink, and she'd scorched 3 gallons of the stuff. And she was still only half done!

Such experiences have made her a fan of small-batch canning—small yields of up to 6 pints or maybe 6 quarts per batch. Anything more than that and canning fatigue sets in. Of course, if you want to preserve an entire plum tree, by all means go for it, but the recipes in this book are scaled for those who don't have time or necessarily space to put up such a large haul. Kelly's recipes can be completed in 2 to 4 hours, tops, so you can get on with the rest of your day.

2. MAKE ONLY STUFF YOU ACTUALLY *WANT* TO EAT

Sounds obvious, right? Yet sometimes canners end up preserving stuff simply because they can't bear to waste any fresh fruits and vegetables. Many times Jessie has made exotic-sounding recipes with names like Tropical Island Thunder simply because the main ingredient, the humble green bell pepper, was one that her back-yard garden produced in spades—only to discover she had no interest in eating the stuff 6 months later. She couldn't pawn it off on friends, thus risk tarnishing her "canner's cred," and she couldn't bring herself to throw it out because of the work involved, so . . . she was stuck with it. To this day, at least eight jars of Tropical Island Thunder haunt her pantry.

In such predicaments, sometimes it makes more sense *not* to can and instead just to eat the excess produce, freeze it, or, as Jessie has done, shove it in a plastic bag and drop it on your neighbor's doorstep accompanied by a note from the "bell pepper fairy."

The recipes in *Tart and Sweet* focus first and foremost on selections that taste *best* when canned—you won't find any strange green bell pepper repositories here.

3. INVEST IN THE RIGHT GEAR

Trying to fish a flat metal lid from a pot of boiling water with a pair of tongs requires the dexterity of your grandma. And you're not your grandma. You're a postmillennial canner who in all likelihood can benefit from using the right tools for the job. But think of it this way—having the right tools makes the job not only more efficient but safer. See page 9 for what gear is a must-have and what you don't need.

4. KNOW WHAT YOU CAN AND CAN'T TWEAK IN A RECIPE

Although the USDA recommends never altering a canning recipe—which could create an environment for bacteria to grow—let's be honest, some cooks do it anyway.

Exhibit A: When Jessie first started canning years ago, she made quarts and quarts of salsa of her own creation that, in hindsight, didn't contain nearly enough acid to ensure that microorganisms were destroyed. Luckily, the salsa turned out fine. But playing fast and loose with acidity levels could have resulted in food poisoning. So while we don't suggest altering any of the canning recipes here, if you must tweak, see page 21 for what you can and absolutely cannot alter.

5. DON'T SWEAT IT IF A JAR FAILS TO SEAL

Chances are, it's not your fault. A faulty lid was probably to blame. Just process it again (see page 20 for instructions). Or simply refrigerate it and consume the contents within a year.

6. YIELDS AREN'T SET IN STONE

The age, size, and water content of your produce may differ substantially from what we used during the testing phase of each recipe, so your yield may turn out to be more or less than what's given. As a general rule, prepare more canning jars and lids than a recipe calls for, since it's better to be overprepared than to come up short.

7. YOU COULD CAN ALONE—BUT WHY?

Canning with friends is the best part of preserving. You get to hang out, laugh, share canning tips and tricks, and eat garden fresh food. And since everyone shares in the food prep and the packing and boiling of jars, the workload is spread around equally. So you can preserve larger volumes quicker . . . and break for cocktails earlier. Is there a better way to spend a Saturday afternoon? Jessie and Kelly submit no. In fact, cocktails and canning are wonderful in combination, since pickles and preserved fruits make the best drink garnishes. In Chapter 9, we show you how to host a killer canning party and offer a selection of yummy cocktail recipes to serve your guests.

Now, let's get canning!

What Is Canning? (Prepare Yourself for a Little Canning Science)

At its essence, home canning is about halting the natural process of deterioration in food. This is done by heating the food to a specific temperature for a specific amount of time to destroy the microorganisms that would otherwise turn to enzymes, bacteria, mold, and yeast if left unpreserved. This is why your canning area, canning utensils and equipment, as well as the food itself, should be as clean as possible so you don't inadvertently introduce more germs to what you're trying to de-germ.

There are two types of canning: water bath canning—which means jars are placed in a pot of boiling water (a technique referred to as "processing" from here on out)—and pressure canning. Which method you choose depends on the acidity of the food you are canning. High-acid food may be boiled in a water bath or pressure canned, but low-acid food must, must, *must* be pressure canned. As previously mentioned, the recipes in this book that require heat processing use the water bath canning method.

What is high- or low-acid food? High-acid food has an acidity level—known as a pH—of 4.6 or lower. The acid it contains is either naturally occurring, like in fruit, or added, like in vinegar. The addition of an acidifying agent such as vinegar provides enough acid to make otherwise low-acid vegetables like asparagus or okra safe for water bath canning—they become pickled. (Plain asparagus and plain okra, on the other hand, must be pressure canned.) For produce such as tomatoes that can straddle the line between high acid and low, lemon (or lime) juice or citric acid is added to ensure there's enough acid present for the food to be processed in a water bath. All fruit (except for figs), fruit spreads, acidified tomatoes (see page 38), pickles, relishes, and chutneys—the mouthwatering deliciousness you'll find within these pages—fall into the high-acid category.

Low-acid food, on the other hand, refers to food that has a pH of 4.6 or higher. (It's confusing—the *lower* the acid, the *higher* the pH; the *higher* the acid, the *lower* the pH.) All meats, poultry, seafood, dairy, and plain nonpickled vegetables fall into this category. These foods contain insufficient acid to prevent the growth of bacteria, including the potentially fatal *Clostridium botulinum*. *C. botulinum* (botulism) is a particularly scary form of food poisoning because it often has no taste or smell—you won't even know you're eating it until . . . it's too late. Botulinum spores are found on most fresh foods and are perfectly safe to eat. They can only reproduce—that is, become deadly—in an *airless*, moist, room-temperature, low-acid environment like that inside a sealed canning jar. This is why all low-acid food must be heated to a much higher temperature—240°F—to ensure the food is safe to eat. This temperature can't be reached under normal boiling conditions, so pressure must be added using a pressure canner, a more complicated process we have opted to save for another cookbook.

HIGH-ACID CANNING

The great thing about canning high-acid food is that acid is a natural sterilizing agent; it blunts the growth of the four spoilers—enzymes, bacteria, molds, and yeasts. It does not, however, destroy them completely—an open jar of relish left at room temperature will definitely get funky after a while. Which is why in addition to acid, a high temperature is necessary to prevent spoilers from flourishing. Spoilers thrive in warm, moist environments, but they can't withstand intense heat. In fact, they're destroyed at a temperature of 212°F—which happens to be the temperature of boiling water at sea level. This is why sealed canning jars are processed in a pot of water for a specific amount of time. Processing time is determined by how long it takes to heat the "cold spot" in the jar, the area that takes the longest to heat, which depends on the chunkiness and viscosity of the food. Chunky pickled beets, for example, will process longer than thinner blueberry lemongrass syrup. Processing is also essential for the creation of the airtight seal—the third line of defense against spoilers. Microorganisms can't survive in the absence of air. As the food heats up inside the jars, pressure builds, forcing air out. This creates a vacuum inside the jar, causing the rubberized flange on the lid to suck down onto the jar and create a seal. This buildup and release of pressure recurs continually, even after the jar is removed from the canner and allowed to cool; eventually all the air is expelled from inside the jar, and an airtight seal is formed.

So a recap of the three things responsible for preserving food in water bath canning:

One, the amount of acid in the food itself blunts the growth of microorganisms. **Two,** processing the jars in boiling water heats the food enough to destroy remaining microorganisms. **Three,** boiling and then cooling the jars creates a vacuum inside the jars so there's no risk the food will become recontaminated by air. The food is now preserved.

ALTITUDE

Altitude plays an important role in canning, because the temperature at which water boils decreases as elevation increases. At sea level, water boils at 212°F, which is hot enough to kill spoilers lurking in high-acid food. If you are at a higher altitude, your water will boil at a lower temperature, which means you have to process the jars longer.

The recipes in this book were calibrated for processing at sea level—they were concocted in a Brooklyn kitchen—which is anywhere from zero to 1,000 feet. Additional time must be added by you when preserving at higher elevations. How to find your elevation? Doing a quick Internet search of your city's name and the word *elevation* should reveal the answer, or you can go to your town's official Web site and search by city data. But definitely take the time to find out this information. You may be surprised by your town's elevation, even if you're in the middle of the country. (Did you know the elevation of Goodland, Kansas—*Kansas*—is a nosebleed-worthy 3,683 feet?)

Altitude Adjustments for Water Bath Processing

IF YOUR ALTITUDE (IN FEET) IS...	INCREASE PROCESSING TIME BY...
1,001–3,000	5 minutes
3,001–6,000	10 minutes
6,001–8,000	15 minutes
8,001–10,000	20 minutes

CANNING GEAR

On the following page, we've outlined which supplies and tools are a must. In the interest of keeping costs down, we've also listed which ones you probably don't need and suggested a few extras that might make canning more enjoyable.

The Acidity (pH) of Popular Canning Ingredients

- **0 = Pure acid**
- 2 = Lemon juice, lime juice
- 2–3 = Damson plums, gooseberries, grapes, rhubarb, vinegar
- 3 = Apples, apricots, blueberries, grapefruit, plums, raspberries, sauerkraut, strawberries, tomatillos
- 3–4 = Blackberries, cherries, kumquats, mangoes, nectarines, oranges, peaches, pears, tangerines
- 4 = Tomatoes
- 4.6 = THE LINE BETWEEN HIGH ACID AND LOW
- 4–5 = Bananas, pumpkin, squash
- 5 = Cauliflower, cucumbers, figs, onions, turnips, watermelon
- 5–6 = Beans, beets, cabbage, carrots, eggplant, okra, zucchini
- 6 = Asparagus, corn, mushrooms, peas
- **14 = Pure alkaline**

(Data from the US Food and Drug Administration, 2007)

Essentials

LARGE POT: Either a regular kitchen pot or canner is fine. Look for one that holds at least 8 quarts. The taller the pot, the better it is for processing quart jars.

SMALL POT (1 TO 2 QUARTS): Needed for preheating lids.

RACK: Necessary for circulating water underneath the jars in the pot, otherwise the jars might shatter. Canners are equipped with racks. If you don't have one or are using a regular kitchen pot, do as Kelly does and place a dish towel in the bottom of the pot or substitute a round aluminum or stainless steel cake rack.

CANNING JARS: The USDA recommends using only jars made specifically for canning, such as those made by Ball, Kerr, or Mason—not old mayonnaise or pickle jars. Your canning jars should come with two-piece metal closures (the old-school style featuring wire bails and glass caps is pretty but may not work as well). There is also the Weck jar, a popular style of canning jar in Europe featuring a rubber ring and lid secured by two spring clamps, but Weck is not endorsed by the USDA, even though canning with them is perfectly safe. We like Weck jars because they're prettier than Ball jars, but they can be harder to find and are rather pricey. For all types of canning jars, sizes range from 4 ounces to 1 quart. You'll find you will use half-pint (8 ounces), pint (16 ounces), and quart (32 ounces) jars most frequently (see Measurement Equivalents on page 14 for converting pints to quarts, etc.). Half-gallons are available, but they're too tall for most canners and are recommended only for highly acidic juices anyway. Canning jars come with regular or wide-mouth openings. Both work well, but if we had to pick just one, we'd go with wide-mouth jars, which are great for canning whole fruits and vegetables, as well as spreads and sauces.

SCREW BANDS AND LIDS: These come with all new jars. You can also buy them separately wherever canning gear is sold. Screw bands can be used forever, while flat metal lids can be used only once (see page 17 for more information)—in other words, you have to use a new lid each time you can.

MAGNETIC WAND: Essentially a magnet on a stick, a wand retrieves metal lids submerged in hot water. (Lids tend to stick together in hot water, and trying to retrieve them with regular tongs is cumbersome.)

JAR LIFTER: Rubber-coated tongs contoured to give you a secure grip as you lift and lower jars in and out of the canner.

LADLE: For pouring food into the jars.

FUNNEL(S): Hot sugar can make a big mess. Sized for regular and wide-mouth jars, funnels prevent food from splashing on the outside of the jars . . . or on you.

PLENTY OF CLEAN DISH TOWELS OR PAPER TOWELS: For wiping down rims of unsealed jars. You can also set jars on dish towels (or a cutting board or other heat-resistant surface) right after processing to prevent the risk of breakage.

All in One

Get all your gear at once with a home canning kit. These typically include a water canner, a rack, tools, a few jars, and even some recipes. Check out canning kits at Amazon, Target, or canningpantry.com.

Canning Costs

Like any other DIY craft—sewing, knitting, home brewing—canning requires a few things to get started. Thankfully, most all your costs occur up front and drop by the second season. To give a sense of what's involved, here's a general cost breakdown for a first-time canner versus someone who's been doing it a couple of years, both of whom are making pickles from farm stand cucumbers.

	NEW CANNER	SEASONED CANNER
Canning pot	$40	Already owns
Pint jars (case)	$11	Already owns
Tool kit	$15	Already owns
Pickle brine ingredients (vinegar, spices, etc.)	$10	$5 (a seasoned canner usually has at least some of the ingredients)
New lids	$3	$3
3 pounds cucumbers	$6	$6
Ballpark total	**$85**	**$14**

Note: Costs decrease more than 70 percent after the first year's canning.

Nonessentials

AIR BUBBLE REMOVER: Facilitates the release of trapped air bubbles in jars prior to sealing. A plain butter knife or a long, thin rubber spatula will suffice.

JAR WRENCHER: For prying lids off jars after they've sealed; the underside of a metal spoon is a fine substitute.

Extras

KITCHEN SCALE AND MEASURING CUP(S): For ensuring precise measurements.

IMMERSION BLENDER: Conveniently purees fruit butters and spreads in the pot without having to transfer contents to a stand blender.

KITCHEN TIMER: Key for accurately and conveniently gauging processing times.

MICROPLANE: Allows for finer grating and zesting than a standard grater.

MANDOLINE: Great for making uniform slices and cuts. And food doesn't get mushy, which can sometimes happen when using a food processor.

FOOD MILL OR STRAINER: Great for seeding tomatoes and berries for sauces and spreads.

CHEESECLOTH: Finely woven fabric frequently used to strain seeds or cut into small swatches to be made into spice bags.

HIGH-PRESSURE OUTDOOR COOKER: Think of it as canning alfresco. Consists of a single burner welded into a portable steel frame that hooks up to a propane tank, enabling you to can outside. (No steamy windows, no omnipresent pickle smell on your couch!) Also, high-pressure burners are capable of reaching much hotter temperatures more quickly than conventional stove tops, which means considerably less time standing around waiting for water to boil. Some municipalities such as New York City require consumers to get a permit before operating a propane tank, so check with your local propane company or city code compliance office to find out what the local rules are. Find outdoor gas cookers at cooking.com, williamsbrewing.com, or Amazon.

How Many Cups Are in a Quart . . . And Other Measurement Questions Answered

Use this chart to convert teaspoons to tablespoons, cups to pints, and pints to quarts.

	TEASPOON	TABLESPOON	¼ CUP	CUP	PINT	QUART
Teaspoon(s)	1	3	12	48	96	192
Tablespoon(s)		1	4	16	32	64
¼ cup(s)			1	4	8	16
Cup(s)				1	2	4
Pint(s)					1	2
Quart(s)						1

Quality Control

Home preserving is a very simple process, but there are a few guidelines to keep in mind in regard to the quality of the food, proper care of your equipment, and specific techniques that will ensure that the craft remains safe and fun. Read the following before embarking on a jamming journey or pickling odyssey.

THE FOOD

It's worth remembering: Canning doesn't improve the quality of produce; it just preserves its current condition. So try to can only the freshest, ripest fruits and vegetables, ideally in their purest, most natural forms—meaning those grown without the use of pesticides and fungicides (who wants to preserve those icky things?)

and not treated with wax to preserve shelf life (such as cucumbers from the grocery store). If you're using produce that has been treated with wax, thoroughly scrub it in hot water to remove as much chemical waxy residue as possible before canning.

A word about organic food: While it's true that organic produce is a bit more labor intensive to grow and therefore more expensive (but thankfully becoming less so all the time), it's worth it to can. Think of it this way—you're saving the good stuff for later. There will always be a waxy cucumber or pesticide-coated apple waiting for you at the grocery store in February. Canned peaches from a backyard tree? A little harder to come by; a little more precious. Reserve the most pristine fruits and vegetables for your canning jars so that you can enjoy them year round.

Accordingly, toss any insect-damaged, diseased, moldy, or overripe fruits and veggies into the garbage or compost heap. Ideally, vegetables should be canned between 6 and 12 hours after being picked, while fruits such as nectarines, peaches, pears, plums, and apricots achieve their juiciest flavor a day after being picked. Wash all produce well in warm water and cut away any blemishes or bruises. Refrigerate fruits and vegetables that can't be canned right away.

THE POT

Sometimes if you've been canning a lot, you may notice a buildup of hard water on the inside of the pot—mineral deposits that won't wash away. To get rid of it, soak the inside of the pot in a solution of 1 cup vinegar to 1 gallon water for an hour or so, then wash and rinse as usual.

Another pot issue: In order for lids to seal properly, jars need to be submerged by at least an inch of water, preferably 2, when the water is at a full rolling boil. In a perfect world, the water level should be 3 inches deeper than the height of the jars to allow for 2 inches of evaporation (it's surprising how quickly water evaporates when you're in the throes of canning . . . especially if you're a newbie). This is why it's not a bad idea to keep a smaller, secondary pot of boiling water, such as a teakettle, on hand.

THE JARS

Wash jars in hot, soapy water or in the dishwasher and rinse well. Jars should be free of nicks or scratches, which are breeding grounds for bacteria. If you notice any hard-water film on older jars (the film will give the glass a cloudy appearance), soak them for a couple of hours in a solution of 1 cup vinegar per 1 gallon water (or reduce the amount to $\frac{1}{2}$ cup vinegar per 2 quarts water).

The USDA says jars don't need to be sterilized *unless* what you're canning has a processing time of under 10 minutes. But we think that since you're already bringing a pot of water to a boil, why not stick the jars in and sterilize them anyway? A 10-minute soak in boiling water is enough, adding an extra minute for every 1,000-foot increase in elevation. Another benefit of sterilizing jars: Presoaking them in hot water prevents thermal shock, a condition that could occur when boiling liquid is poured into a room temperature or cool jar, which may cause it to shatter.

THE SCREW BANDS AND LIDS

As we mentioned earlier, screw bands can be used forever, while flat lids can be used only once. The reason lids are single use is because the rim of the lid is coated

with a food-safe sealing compound—a gasket. During processing, the sealant softens to "wrap" the rim of the jar, forming an airtight seal. Because it changes shape during processing, it cannot reseal to a second jar.

No need to throw used lids away, however. They can be used again to contain short-term perishables (sauces, refrigerator pickles) or nonperishables. Use a Sharpie to mark used lids so that you know not to use them again for canning.

HEADSPACE—MORE THAN JUST A STATE OF MIND

Headspace refers to the unfilled space at the top of the jar—the empty space between the top of the food and the bottom of the lid. Headspace is important because it gives food room to expand during processing. The extent to which food expands depends on the amount of air contained in it as well as processing time and temperature. The greater the processing time, the more food expands. The less the processing time, the less it expands. Also, headspace is key for the proper formation of a vacuum seal as the jar cools. In other words, headspace is very important. Don't mess with headspace. The measurements below will help you determine how much headspace you need to leave in your jar. See the opposite page for a visual reference.

Headspace requirements for water bath canning:

SOFT SPREADS (JAMS AND JELLIES): $\frac{1}{4}$ inch headspace

FRUITS, TOMATOES, PICKLES, RELISHES, CHUTNEYS, CONDIMENTS: $\frac{1}{2}$ inch headspace

PACKING TECHNIQUES

There are two ways to pack produce into jars—raw pack and hot pack. Both have their advantages and disadvantages.

In **raw packing,** jars are filled with raw, unheated food that is topped with hot liquid. The jars are then sealed and processed. Raw packing is great for preserving more delicate foods such as asparagus, which can turn to mush if precooked. And since the food isn't cooked first, raw packing generally makes for faster canning.

PICKLES
½ INCH

JAMS
¼ INCH

The downside is that less food fits into jars. Plus raw food contains more air than cooked food, which can potentially compromise the seal of the jar if the food isn't canned properly.

For **hot packing,** jars are filled with food, such as halved or whole peaches, that's already been lightly cooked. Cooking the food helps to draw air from its tissues and shrink its overall volume. The warm food is then covered with hot liquid, and the jars are sealed and processed. Not only does hot packing allow you to fit more food into the jar, it also helps preserve color and flavor a bit better than a raw pack. The downside is that hot packing takes longer and usually means another pot to wash. You'll see both methods used in the book, though we usually opt for the raw packing because it's a bit faster and helps the food retain a better texture.

TESTING THE SEALS

Once the jars have been processed, they need time to cool. The cooling period is important, since that's when the vacuum seal is formed. So try not to handle the jars excessively for 12 hours or so (now is not the time to play a game of hot potato—or hot pickles—with them).

Usually, you can tell a jar has sealed if you hear a *ping!* sound—which signifies that the last bit of air has been sucked from the jar and an airtight seal has formed. But since you don't always hear the ping, there are a few other ways to check.

- Press down on the center of the lid with your finger. If there's no give—if the lid doesn't pop up upon release of your finger—it's sealed.

- Look at the jar at eye level. If the lid is slightly concave (curved down slightly), it's sealed. If it's flat or bulging, it's not.

- Remove the screw band and gently try to pry the lid off with your fingers. If it doesn't budge, it's sealed.

What to Do If a Jar Fails to Seal

This rarely happens, but when it does, we usually just refrigerate the jars and treat the contents like any other perishable (we eat 'em).

Jars can be reprocessed using the original processing instructions in the recipe, but sometimes it's more trouble than it's worth, given that usually only one or

Tweaking a Recipe to Your Liking

The USDA doesn't recommend modifying canning recipes, since improvising could affect the acidity of your canned goods and create an environment for bacteria to thrive. But as any cook knows, half the fun of making a recipe more than once is the tweaking! We've discovered that there are a handful of key changes you can make safely.

SUGAR. Feel free to add more or less. It's only added for flavor and to help stabilize the shape, set, and color of whatever it is you're canning. It's not added as a preservative. Keep in mind, though, that insufficient amounts of sugar in jams and fruit spreads will result in a runny, dribbly spread, which can sometimes—but not always—be remedied by increasing the cooking time or by adding more pectin.

SALT. Feel free to add more or less except when making fermented canned goods. In canning recipes, salt is used for flavor only and doesn't affect spoilage. It will, however, affect texture and crunch. Salt pulls moisture from food; too little salt can make a mushy, water-logged pickle. Be sure to use only salts labeled "kosher," "canning," or "pickling," since regular table salt will make your brine cloudy.

SALSA. When making salsa, you can substitute one type of pepper for another, as long as you don't increase the total amount.

LEMON OR LIME JUICE. If you prefer the flavor, you can substitute bottled lemon or bottled lime juice for vinegar. Unless otherwise noted, always stick to bottled citrus juices, since fresh can vary in acidity.

HERBS AND SPICES. Feel free to play with the amounts of herbs and spices called for in a recipe—it won't adversely affect the recipe's pH.

VINEGAR. It's okay to substitute one kind of vinegar for another as long as the vinegar you choose is at least 5 percent acid. You can find this information on the bottle.

HONEY. Honey can be substituted for sugar, though keep in mind that it's not a cup-for-cup conversion, since honey is more dense than granulated sugar.

A few changes never to make:

Never increase the amount of vegetables. This could push the pH into dangerously low-acid territory.

Never decrease the amount of acid, whether vinegar, lime juice, or lemon juice.

Never substitute vinegar for bottled lemon or lime juice in a recipe, since vinegar is slightly less acidic than the citruses.

Never add more water than a recipe calls for. This could dilute the acidity to unsafe levels.

Never tweak the amount of salt in a fermented pickle recipe (such as kimchi or sauerkraut). Too little salt can cause undesirable organisms to grow; too much can kill the beneficial lactic acid bacteria, which is what preserves the food.

two jars fail to seal. Plus, excessive processing (boiling the jars a second time) can diminish flavor and quality. If you opt to reprocess, do it within 24 hours. Double-check the condition of the jar to make sure it's free of any scratches or hairline cracks. Make sure the headspace is accurate. Check that the sealant on the underside of the lid is free of nicks. You may decide to swap out for a whole new lid and jar and try again.

PRESERVING YOUR PRESERVES

You can store canned goods wherever you have room, but the ideal location is in a cool, dark place. A cool temperature—anywhere in the 50° to 70°F range—helps slow down vitamin loss of the food in the jars. Darkness prevents the food from losing its color due to sunlight or artificial light. We like to label and date our jars and store them wherever we can admire them and, more important, remember them—such as in the pantry or cupboard.

However, there is one teensy drawback to proudly displaying your canned goods: Friends and family have a tendency to take them. We know you're supposed to want to share your homemade seasonal goods—and we share dozens of jars of them—but we have found that putting up quarts and quarts of homegrown tomato sauce for the winter can induce a kind of canner's hoarding mentality hastened by friends' assumption that because you have so many, surely you won't mind if they take a jar home. If you, like us, have a deep connection to your canned goods, keep an eye on your jars.

CAN -TASTROPHES

As we've mentioned, the official shelf life of unopened canned food is 1 year. After that point, the flavor, nutritional quality, color, and texture of the food begin to diminish. That said, we've cracked open plenty of pints of ketchup and jars of chutney or peaches a year and a half after preserving them, and they tasted fine—so it's really a matter of personal choice. Use your judgment; if the contents look weird—emerging blemishes, an unnatural darkening of color—they probably *are* weird. Don't eat them. Treat spoiled canned goods as you would any other icky food—throw them in the trash. Jars can be thoroughly cleaned and used again.

While we're on the subject . . .

How to Tell Your Canned Food Is Destined for the Dumpster

The following indicators are all telltale signs your jarred bounty has spoiled.

- **A BULGING LID:** Spoilage bacteria and yeast produce gas, which pressurizes the food, priming the lid to explode—it's like Chernobyl in a Mason jar.

- **RISING AIR BUBBLES IN THE JAR:** This means the food is building pressure, the result of spoiler buildup.

- **COTTONLIKE MOLD GROWTH ON TOP OF THE FOOD OR ON THE UNDERSIDE OF THE LID:** Not only is mold gross, but it can raise the pH of the food, making it dangerously low acid, and therefore running the risk of botulism or other bacterial spoilage. Scraping mold off canned food does not make it safe—throw it out.

- **A CHANGE OF TEXTURE:** Specifically, to a slimy one.

- **THE BIGGIE:** A bad smell upon opening.

- **THE ULTIMATE BIGGIE:** Spurting liquid upon opening.

Water Bath Canning, Step-by-Step

Now that you know a little about the science of canning and what equipment you need, you're ready to begin preserving!

Before you start cooking up a pot of raspberries destined for jam, take a few minutes to read through the following steps so you know exactly what to expect each step of the way—because once you start canning, things tend to move quickly.

Keep in mind that you'll need three burners—one for processing the jars, one for preheating the flat lids, and one for cooking the recipe. (You may even need a fourth burner for a secondary pot of boiling water should evaporation become an issue.)

1. ASSEMBLE YOUR EQUIPMENT

As with any type of cooking, prep is key. Get out your pot and rack, jars and lids—it's a good idea to prepare a few more jars than you think you need, just in case—and all the necessary canning tools: magnetic wand, funnels, jar lifter, dish towels, cutting board, etc. Wash the produce, sharpen your knives, read through the recipe, and line up whatever ingredients and spices the recipe calls for.

2. CLEAN THE JARS AND TOPS

If you're using old jars, be on the lookout for any nicks and scratches (breeding grounds for bacteria) and replace defective vessels with new ones. Wash canning jars, lids, and screw bands in hot soapy water or run them through the dishwasher. Remember, flat metal lids must be *new*, since used ones won't reseal to jars.

3. HEAT THE WATER

Place the empty jars without their lids in a large pot equipped with a rack (if you don't have a rack, use a dish towel—anything to keep the bottoms of the jars from making direct contact with the bottom of the pot) and fill with enough water so that the jars—once sealed and put back into the pot—are covered by 2 inches of water. In other words, fill with more water than you think you need. Bring the water to a boil. This not only heats the water for processing but sterilizes the jars. If your water comes to a rolling boil before you're finished preparing the recipe, reduce the heat

to low and then bring it back to high once you're closer to being ready. This way, you don't waste time waiting around for water to boil, the number one time-drain for canners.

4. PREPARE THE LIDS

As the jars warm up, heat the lids in a small saucepan of water over low heat using the simmer burner on your stove. Don't allow the water to boil, since this might interfere with the sealing compound. While it's not crucial to heat the screw bands, it's nice to have everything as sterile and clean as possible.

5. MAKE THE RECIPE

Cook or prepare your food as directed by the recipe.

6. FILL THE JARS

Once the recipe is ready, use a pair of canning tongs to retrieve the hot jars from the canning water. Turn the jars upside down so the water pours back into the pot. Set the wet empty jars on a cutting board, dish towel, or other heat-protected surface.

- Ladle in the food, allowing for headspace. It's helpful to use a funnel to prevent splashing.

- Slide a narrow rubber spatula or butter knife down the side of the jar a few times to release trapped pockets of air. For chunkier foods, like pickles, you can also tap the bottom of the jar on the counter a few times to release trapped air. Air bubbles can cause seal failure, so it's important not to skip this step.

- Use a clean dish towel or paper towel to wipe down the rim of the jar. Otherwise, tiny food particles here may prevent a seal and provide an opening for air (bacteria) to get in.

- Use a magnetic wand or tongs to retrieve a flat lid from the smaller pot of water. Carefully place it over the mouth of the jar, making sure the gasket covers the rim. Place a screw band on the jar and firmly tighten. Not too tight. Overtightening can prevent air from escaping during processing and lead to seal failure. Undertightening may cause the lid to slip, which could also lead to seal failure. Repeat this process until all the jars are sealed.

- Place the sealed jars in the pot of boiling water. Try not to cram them in there—you should be able to lift the jars easily in and out of the pot. Cover the pot with a lid.

7. HEAT-PROCESS THE JARS

Once the jars are in the covered pot and the water is at a full boil, start the clock for processing, adjusting for elevation.

8. COOL THE JARS

After the jars have processed, turn off the heat and wait for the water to stop bubbling before removing the jars. Place the jars on a cooling rack or a heat-absorbent surface, such as a towel or cutting board, allowing for space so air can freely circulate between them. Leave them undisturbed until they're cool to the touch.

9. CHECK THE SEALS

After the jars have cooled completely (up to 8 hours or so), eyeball the lids. If the lid is concave—curved downward—the jar has sealed. To check, press your finger into the center of the lid. If there's no give—if it doesn't pop up upon release of your finger—it's airtight.

10. LABEL AND STORE THEM

If the jars are sticky—the result of canning liquid seeping out during processing—wipe them down with a damp cloth. Label and date the contents. Stash in a cool, dark place.

3

Fruit Spreads
and Tomatoes

The ingredients that make up fruit spreads—jams, jellies, conserves, fruit butters—are fairly straightforward: fresh fruit and

sugar. They can be combined with all sorts of heady spices and herbs and piquant flavorings, but these two key ingredients remain sublimely simple. So the trick to perfecting a fruit spread is achieving the right "set"—the right jammy, spreadable, buttery, wobbly consistency, depending on the type of preserve you're making. A spread's consistency boils down to four players: fruit, acid, pectin, and sugar. These components must be in the right balance for each type of spread to achieve the consistency you're aiming for.

Fruit

Fruit used for making preserves should be perfectly ripe. Overripe fruit, by contrast, contains less pectin and less acid, which could affect the overall acidity level, making it less safe to can. Using overripe fruit also affects the ability of the finished product to set properly. As with all types of canning, seek out the freshest produce available, ideally organically grown and locally sourced, and wash it well.

Acid

All fruits, except for figs, bananas, and watermelons, are high acid (refer to the acidity chart on page 9 for more details). Acid (along with heat processing) is the key preservative in fruit, combating the growth of microorganisms. Acid is also responsible for preserving the bright color and flavor of fruit and is necessary for fruit preserves to form a gel. If there is too little acid, the gel will be runny. If there's too much acid, the gel will lose liquid, or "weep." When canning fruits lower in acid, such as blueberries, additional high-acid fruit or acid in the form of bottled lemon juice is usually added to hasten gelling.

Pectin

Pectin is a natural fiber found in varying degrees in the tissue, skin, and seeds of fruit (and some vegetables). When combined with sugar and acid, it binds to form a gumlike consistency (refer to the pectin chart to find the amounts of pectin contained in common canning fruits). Pectin is what allows fruit spreads to set. Cooking releases pectin, but cooking too long may destroy it. High-pectin fruits, such as apples and currants, produce a spread that sets easily. Low-pectin fruits, such as strawberries and raspberries, may need a little help, either by extending the cooking time to hasten thickening (but not too long!) or by adding other high-pectin fruits to the mix (combining strawberries with apples, for example). You can also use commercially produced liquid or powdered pectin. To create fruit preserves with a firm consistency, like jelly, more pectin is needed. For a looser consistency, like jam, less pectin is needed.

These days there are many commercial pectins available that are "low-methoxyl," meaning the gelling power is activated by calcium, not sugar. Examples include Sure-Jell Pectin for Less or No Sugar Needed Recipes, Mrs. Wages Lite Home-Jell, or Pomona's Universal Pectin. Sure-Jell's low-sugar pectin and Mrs. Wages Lite pectin include calcium *in* the pectin, as well as a bit of sugar, so all you do is add the pectin to the recipe as directed. Pomona's Universal Pectin, which includes no sugar whatsoever and is therefore the one we use most frequently in the recipes, takes an extra step to prepare (see "Pomona's Universal Pectin" on page 34 for more details).

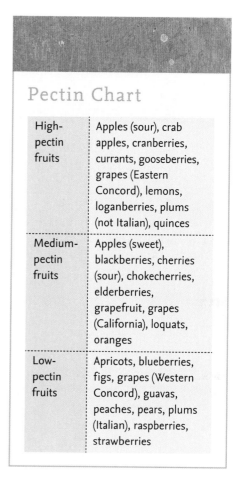

Pectin Chart

High-pectin fruits	Apples (sour), crab apples, cranberries, currants, gooseberries, grapes (Eastern Concord), lemons, loganberries, plums (not Italian), quinces
Medium-pectin fruits	Apples (sweet), blackberries, cherries (sour), chokecherries, elderberries, grapefruit, grapes (California), loquats, oranges
Low-pectin fruits	Apricots, blueberries, figs, grapes (Western Concord), guavas, peaches, pears, plums (Italian), raspberries, strawberries

Sugar

Although sugar exhibits some preserving qualities, it is not, as we've mentioned, a key preservative in canned foods. A sufficient amount of acid, combined with heat processing, is what ultimately preserves fruit. Sugar is added to improve flavor, stabilize color, retain texture, and help form a gel. However, heavily sugared fruit spreads will have a longer shelf life *once opened* than their less- or no-sugar counterparts.

Pomona's Universal Pectin

Though it may seem as if we're giving Pomona's special attention in the recipes, it's not intentional. The product is the only no-sugar pectin we know of, so it's the one we end up using in the recipes!

Each box includes a little packet of calcium powder that must be made into calcium water before it can be added to the recipe, followed by the pectin.

To make the calcium water, combine ½ teaspoon of calcium powder and ½ cup of water. Add the appropriate amount of calcium water that the recipe calls for, then add the recommended amount of pectin powder and cook as directed. Store the extra calcium water in the refrigerator between uses. (Note: Recipes refer back to these directions.)

Many people today aren't fans of cloyingly sweet preserves, preferring the natural sweetness of the fruit to take center stage, and the recipes in the book reflect that. Most of Kelly's fruit spread recipes call for minimal amounts of sugar. This is why you won't find recipes for jelly—which is pretty much just lots of sugar combined with fruit—in these pages. Jams, fruit butters, preserves, conserves, etc., are all much more forgiving, in terms of both preparation and nutrition. You can add a little bit more sugar to any of the fruit preserves in this book if you prefer a sweeter flavor, but keep in mind as you taste a spoonful of your mixture that the preserves will taste sweeter after they cool.

To make a fruit spread that does not contain excess sugar or added pectin, the recipe must either be cooked longer to thicken and reach the desired consistency or include fruits that are naturally high acid and/or high pectin.

Testing Fruit Spreads for Doneness

You may have paired nature's finest raspberries with just a hint of sugar and other flavorings to make the world's best jam, but making perfect fruit preserves all boils down to nailing that elusive set—knowing *when* it's time to ladle your luscious creation into the jar. To help you achieve a prizewinning preserve, we offer you four time-honored methods to test for doneness.

1. THE CHILLED PLATE TEST

Pour a bit of the fruit spread onto a plate and stick it in the freezer for a few minutes. When you take the plate out, check to see if any juice has separated from the pulp. (Alternatively, you can chill a plate in the freezer and then add a spoonful of preserves to see if it separates.) If separation occurs (see bottom plate in photo on this page), the mixture needs to be cooked more. If it holds its shape (see top plate in photo), it's ready to be ladled into jars.

2. THE COLD SPOON TEST

This is similar to the chilled plate test, but you don't have to dirty a clean plate: Dip a cold metal spoon into the mixture. If the juice separates from the fruit in the spoon, the mixture needs to be cooked more. If it holds its shape, it's ready to be ladled into jars.

3. THE TEMPERATURE TEST

Boil the mixture for the time required by your recipe. Insert a candy/jelly thermometer into the pot, without letting it touch the sides or bottom. When the thermometer reads 220°F, or what's known as the gel temperature, it's ready to be ladled into jars. (Altitude consideration: For every 1,000 feet over sea level, subtract 2° from this temperature. For example, if your elevation is 3,000 feet, the gel temperature is 214°F.)

4. THE SHEET TEST

Dip a spoon into the mixture as it cooks and hold the spoon horizontally over the pot. If the mixture drips off the edge in two or even three separate droplets, like water or syrup, it's not ready; it's still too runny and requires more cooking (and in some cases, more pectin). The mixture is done when it falls in sheets off the spoon—it slides off in one mass with no dripping.

IS IT A JAM . . . A PRESERVE . . . A COMPOTE . . . OR A CONSERVE? A GLOSSARY OF FRUIT SPREADS

JAM: A mixture of lightly softened fruit and sugar boiled long enough to thicken into a fruity mass. The longer the fruit is cooked, the thicker the mixture becomes. Because of jam's looser set, it's more idiotproof than jelly and can be made using considerably less sugar. Jams are versatile and lend themselves to any number of delicious uses. [*photo*: A: *Raspberry Jam*, B: *Grapefruit Honey Jam*]

MARMALADE: A bittersweet jam made from citrus fruit and slices of peel that's cooked long enough for the peel to soften. Marmalades are typically spread on breads and scones and can be used in baking. [*photo*: C: *Meyer Lemon Marmalade*]

CONSERVE: A chunkier jam that includes large pieces of fruit, dried fruits, and other ingredients such as nuts, coconut, or citrus peel. Some conserves can be eaten like jam, while more savory varieties can be used to accompany meats. [not pictured]

PRESERVES: Small, whole fruits (such as berries) or larger fruits cut into big chunks (such as peaches) that are suspended in a soft jelly. Preserves are often spooned over desserts and used in pastries. [*photo*: D: *Plums in Vanilla Syrup*, E: *Candied Kumquats with Cinnamon and Star Anise*]

FRUIT BUTTER: Made by cooking pureed fruit pulp until it has the consistency of applesauce. Butters tend to be lower in sugar than jams and jellies, so they generally call for a longer cooking time. Fruit butters are spread on breads and other foods and can be used as a healthy replacement for oil in some baked goods recipes. [*photo:* F: *Mango Chili Butter*]

COMPOTE: Small chunks of fruit cooked for a shorter amount of time to attain the consistency of a chunky syrup. Compotes are typically spooned over desserts, ice cream, or yogurt. [*photo:* G: *Strawberry Orange Compote*]

SYRUPS: Made by cooking fruit with sugar until the pulp macerates or the mixture is processed with an immersion blender to make it very smooth. Syrups are typically added to drinks (see page 196) and may also be used in baking. [*photo:* H: *Red Currant Syrup*]

Canning Whole Fruit (and Tomatoes)

For many, the motivation to can comes from a real need to preserve an avalanche of produce—those of you lucky enough to have a plum tree in your yard or any of us who find it impossible to resist such bounty at the farmers' market know this is true. Sometimes the easiest way to harness the harvest is to preserve it in its whole (or marginally cut) state.

WHOLE FRUIT

Most fruits contain enough acid to can safely without adding additional acid (except for figs and bananas, which require the addition of bottled lemon juice). While it's perfectly safe to preserve whole fruit in water, the fruit will become soft and dark within a matter of months. To retain optimum color, flavor, and texture, fruit juice or simple syrup is the canning liquid of choice. You can make the canning liquid as sweet or light as you like. White grape juice and apple juice are two of the more commonly used juices. For a more neutral flavor, you can use simple syrup.

To make simple syrup, combine the desired amount of sugar per 1 quart water in a saucepan over medium heat and stir until the sugar dissolves (up to half of the sugar may be replaced by honey). Raise the temperature to high and boil for 5 minutes. Keep warm as needed. Cover and stash any leftover syrup in the refrigerator and bring back to a boil as needed.

SIMPLE SYRUPS

Per 1 quart (4 cups) water, add:

1 CUP SUGAR = EXTRALIGHT SYRUP

4 CUPS SUGAR = HEAVY SYRUP

2 CUPS SUGAR = LIGHT SYRUP

5 CUPS SUGAR = EXTRAHEAVY SYRUP

3 CUPS SUGAR = MEDIUM SYRUP

WHOLE TOMATOES

In canning, tomatoes are treated more like a fruit than a vegetable (they are technically a fruit) in that they should contain enough acid to preserve safely in a water bath. Operative word: *should*. As tomatoes ripen, acidity can drop to potentially unsafe levels, which is why the USDA recommends acidifying canned tomatoes by adding citric acid (vitamin C) or bottled lemon juice to ensure safe canning. Here's how.

ACIDIFYING TOMATOES

PER PINT (2 CUPS): 1 TABLESPOON BOTTLED LEMON JUICE OR ¼ TEASPOON CITRIC ACID

PER QUART (4 CUPS): 2 TABLESPOONS BOTTLED LEMON JUICE OR ½ TEASPOON CITRIC ACID

Ingredient Prep—Fruit Spreads and Whole Fruits (and Tomatoes)

Before you can can your beautiful produce, you'll first need to prepare. Here's an overview of a few basic techniques you'll use time and time again when making many of the recipes in this book.

BLANCHING AND PEELING

Some produce, particularly peaches, nectarines, and tomatoes, needs to be peeled before it is ready for use in a recipe. You don't want random chunks of skin to interfere with an otherwise perfect peach lavender jam or silky smooth tomato puree. To remove the skins with as little waste as possible, the produce is first blanched. Light-colored stone fruits—peaches, nectarines, apricots—will oxidize (darken) without their skins, which isn't an issue if you're continuing to cook them down for a jam or marmalade, but it can look unappetizing on fruit that is canned whole (though oxidized fruit is perfectly safe to eat). To preserve naked fruit's lovely color, it first needs to be dipped in an anti-browning solution before it goes into the canning jar.

To blanch, fill a large bowl with cold water and ice and set aside. Fill a medium to large saucepan with water and bring it to a boil. As the water heats up, use a knife to make an X on the bottom of each piece of fruit or tomato. (The fruit must be ripe for this trick to work.) Use a pair of tongs to dip the fruit or tomato into the boiling water to loosen the skin. Submerge for 10 to 15 seconds at most. Any longer than that and the produce will begin to cook. Remove it from the pot and submerge in ice water. (Or, in the case of peaches, nectarines, plums, apricots, etc., dip them in a bath of acidulated ice water. See Making an Anti-Browning Solution, below.) When the produce is cool enough to handle, peel by pulling the skin away from the X. Cook or can as directed.

MAKING AN ANTI-BROWNING SOLUTION

To prevent oxidation of light-colored fruits, combine three crushed 500-milligram vitamin C tablets per half-gallon (8 cups) of ice water. Use a mortar and pestle or coffee grinder to crush the tablets. Submerge the peeled or cut fruit in the acidulated ice water for 5 minutes or so. Cook or can as directed.

HULLING A STRAWBERRY

Since no one really owns a strawberry huller, the best way to extract the tough, white core at the top of the berry is to push a plastic drinking straw through the bottom of the berry and up through the leafy stem end. This removes both the core and the stem.

PITTING A CHERRY

You can use a cherry pitter (another tool no one but professionals owns) or push a drinking straw through the bottom of the cherry, forcing the pit up and out through the stem end.

SEGMENTING CITRUS FRUIT

Segmenting citrus fruit is not the same as slicing or dividing it. Segmenting refers to removing each section of pulp from its protective membrane. To do this, first cut ½ inch off each end of the fruit. Peel the rind and, carefully following the contours of the fruit with a very sharp paring knife, cut away the outer pith (the white part) while leaving as much pulp intact as possible. Once the rind and pith have been discarded, hold the fruit in one hand over a large pot. Slip the knife between the membrane and one section of fruit to carefully separate the membrane from the pulp, letting the pulp fall into the pot. Do this for each section, until only the membrane "shell" remains. Once you have removed all the sections, squeeze any remaining juice into the pot, being careful not to let any seeds fall in. Discard the seeds and membrane.

STRAINING SEEDS FOR FRUIT SYRUPS AND SPREADS

Cook down the berries or fruit as directed by your recipe. Set a fine sieve over a bowl (if you don't have a sieve, substitute a mesh strainer or, for a finer texture, a strainer lined with cheesecloth). Pour the simmering fruit pulp into the sieve and allow the juice to drip through. Gently press the pulp with a rubber spatula to extract as much juice as possible, but not so hard that you force seeds and skins through. Wipe off the spatula and swipe the underside of the strainer as well, scraping the pulp into the bowl. Discard the seeds and skin. Return the strained pulp to the pot and continue with the recipe.

MAKING A BOUQUET GARNI

Cut a swatch of cheesecloth big enough to fit the herbs and spices called for in the recipe, leaving extra for tying. Bundle the ingredients in the cheesecloth and tie off the top, or secure with kitchen twine, so no ingredients escape. Add the bouquet garni to the recipe as it cooks; remove it before ladling the spice-infused brine or sauce into canning jars.

SCRAPING VANILLA BEAN SEEDS

Halve the bean lengthwise and place it cut side up on a cutting board. Securely holding the split bean in one hand and a knife in the other, run the blade down the length of the bean, pressing down to scrape out the seeds. Add the seeds to the recipe.

Pickles of All Kinds

A Pickle Primer

IS IT A REFRIGERATOR PICKLE? . . .
A FRESH PICKLE? . . . A FERMENTED PICKLE?
A GLOSSARY OF PICKLES

REFRIGERATOR PICKLES: Raw or blanched produce is submerged in a vinegary brine and stashed in the refrigerator for at least 3 days to cure. Refrigerator pickles are relatively short term and should be eaten within a couple of months. [photo: A: *Pickled Endive*]

FRESH-PACK OR QUICK PICKLES: Raw or blanched produce is packed into canning jars and topped with a hot vinegary brine. The jars are then sealed and heat processed in a water bath. Fresh-pack pickles achieve the tastiest flavor when allowed to cure for several weeks before opening. [photo: B: *Mexican Baby Carrots*, C: *Pickled Garlic Scrapes*, D: *Spicy Dill Pickles*, E: *Mexican Sour Gherkins with Lemon Verbena*]

FRUIT PICKLES: Fruit is covered in a sweetened syrup acidified with either lemon juice or vinegar. These pickles can either be stored in the refrigerator for immediate eating or be packed into canning jars and heat processed for longer-term storage. [not pictured]

FERMENTED PICKLES: Produce is preserved at room temperature over a period of weeks in a salty brine. This process draws juices and sugar from the food to

form lactic acid, which preserves the food and gives fermented pickles their characteristic crunch and tangy flavor. *[photo: F: Sauerkraut]*

RELISH: Essentially a pickle that's been chopped up into small bits and cooked before being ladled into jars, relish is a tangy condiment that is used to enliven sandwiches, hot dogs, hamburgers, meats, and salads. *[photo: G: Carrot Jala-peño Relish]*

CHUTNEY: Similar to a relish, only more heavily spiced and cooked longer for a saucier texture. Chutneys often include fruit. Usually served with meats and spicy foods, but delicious on sandwiches or served alongside cheese. *[photo: H: Raisin-Hater's Apple Chutney]*

SALSA: A chunky, spicy sauce made from a variety of vegetables and certain fruits, such as peaches. Salsas are safe for water bath canning only if properly acidified by bottled lime juice or vinegar. Salsas are typically served as dips or used as toppings in Mexican dishes. *[photo: I: Roasted Tomatillo Salsa Verde]*

RECIPES

ONE jar = easy

TWO jars = moderate

THREE jars = more involved

Winter

Cinnamon Blood Orange Marmalade ◊ Grapefruit Honey Jam ◊ Kumquat Marmalade ◊ Meyer Lemon, Orange Blossom, and Honey Marmalade ◊ Citrus Overload Marmalade ◊ Candied Kumquats with Cinnamon and Star Anise ◊ Preserved Lemons ◊ Ginger Key Lime Syrup ◊ Lemon Herb Pickled Garlic ◊ Horseradish Lemon Pepper Sunchokes ◊ Pickled Pearl Cocktail Onions ◊ Kai's Fire Vinegar

Blood oranges look like slightly smaller navel oranges that have been sunburnt—burnished crimson to red peels encasing juicy pulp the color of blood. Their ruby hue makes a beautiful marmalade.

Cinnamon Blood Orange Marmalade

5 pounds blood oranges (see note)
3 cups blood orange juice (see note) or orange juice
Zest and juice of 2 lemons
1½ tablespoons ground cinnamon
2½ cups sugar, divided
1 tablespoon calcium water (see note)
3¼ teaspoons Pomona's Universal Pectin powder

Take 2 pounds of the oranges and cut off both ends to reveal the pulp. (No bitter white pith should remain at the ends.) Quarter the oranges, removing the center pith and seeds. Slice each quarter into very thin wedges and place in a large pot.

Segment the other 3 pounds of oranges using a very sharp paring knife (see page 40 for instructions) and place the segments in the pot.

Add the juice, zest and juice of 2 lemons, cinnamon, and 1 cup of the sugar to the pot. Bring to a boil over medium-high heat, mixing well. Once it's boiling, lower the heat to medium and simmer for 30 to 45 minutes. The fruit should be broken down and the rinds quite soft. Add the calcium water.

In a separate bowl, mix the remaining 1½ cups sugar and the pectin powder until well combined. Pour into the orange mixture. Stir everything to combine. Turn the heat back up to medium-high and bring to a boil once again, stirring often to prevent scorching. Marmalade should thicken in 5 to 10 minutes. Test for doneness using a chilled plate (see page 34).

Ladle the marmalade into hot jars, leaving ¼ inch headspace. Check for air bubbles, wipe the rims, and seal. Process for 10 minutes, adjusting for elevation. YIELD: **5 PINTS**

NOTE: Store-bought citrus is often coated in wax. If that's what you're using, first dip the fruit into boiling water to remove all traces of wax, then scrub well in cold water.

Blood orange juice is available at specialty markets and Italian grocery stores.

To make calcium water, follow the instructions on the package or see page 34.

In order to get this jam to set up properly without adding a lot of sweetener, I use Pomona's Universal Pectin, which contains no added sugar. This allows me to cut by half the amount of sugar called for in most traditional jam recipes, allowing the natural sweetness of the citrus to shine while maintaining a nice, thick jammy consistency. —*Kelly*

Grapefruit Honey Jam

12 Star Ruby grapefruit, peeled and segmented (see page 40)
1 cup sugar
Zest and juice of 2 lemons
2 tablespoons + 1 teaspoon calcium water (see page 34)
1½ cups honey
4 tablespoons Pomona's Universal Pectin powder

Segment all 12 grapefruits into a large pot. You should have about 16 cups of fruit and juice.

Add the sugar and zest and juice of 2 lemons to the pot and bring to a boil over medium-high heat. Cook down for about 45 minutes, stirring frequently. Add the calcium water.

In a separate small bowl, mix the honey with the pectin powder.

Reduce the heat to low and add the honey mixture to the grapefruit. Slowly bring back to a boil, stirring often to prevent scorching. Continue to cook down for 15 to 20 minutes. Check for doneness using a chilled plate (see page 34).

Ladle the jam into hot jars, leaving ¼ inch headspace. Check for air bubbles, wipe the rims, and seal. Process for 10 minutes, adjusting for elevation.
YIELD: **10 HALF-PINTS**

NOTE: For a smoother jam, mash the cut grapefruit and strain the juice; do a few times before cooking the juice.

Think of this marmalade as a gateway preserve: It's a bridge from the monochromatic doldrums of winter—kumquats' growing season—to the sunny days of spring. Its cheery orange color is a promise of warmer days to come.

Kumquat Marmalade

2½ pounds kumquats, sliced into very thin rounds and seeded (see note)
2½ cups sugar, divided
1½ cups orange juice
Juice of 1 lemon
1 teaspoon ground cinnamon
¼ teaspoon grated nutmeg
3 teaspoons calcium water (see page 34)
3½ teaspoons Pomona's Universal Pectin powder

Place the kumquats and 1 cup of the sugar in a medium pot over medium-high heat. As the fruit starts to break down—after about 15 minutes or so—add the orange and lemon juices, cinnamon, and nutmeg. Continue to cook, stirring often, for 45 minutes. Add the calcium water.

In a separate small bowl, combine the pectin powder with the remaining 1½ cups sugar and add to the pot.

Return the mixture to a boil, stirring often. Check for doneness using a chilled plate (see page 34).

Ladle into hot jars, leaving ¼ inch headspace. Check for air bubbles, wipe the rims, and seal. Process for 10 minutes, adjusting for elevation.
YIELD: 5 HALF-PINTS

NOTE: Unlike most other citrus, kumquats are consumed whole—rind and all. The peel is actually the sweetest part of the fruit. It's the fleshy interior that's tart.

This marmalade is somewhat tart and a tad bitter. It's a delicious accompaniment to sweet breads or scones with clotted cream. If you can, try to use raw, local honey in your marmalade. It will have a nuttier and more complex flavor than industrially produced varieties. —Jessie

Meyer Lemon, Orange Blossom, and Honey Marmalade

5½ pounds Meyer lemons, quartered and sliced ⅛ inch thick
1¼–2 cups sugar, to taste
1 cup honey (see note)
Zest and juice of 2 lemons
⅛ cup orange blossom water (see note)
1 teaspoon vanilla extract
1 teaspoon kosher salt
1 teaspoon ground cinnamon or ½ teaspoon grated ginger (optional)

Place the lemons, sugar, honey, zest and juice of 2 lemons, orange blossom water, vanilla extract, salt, and cinnamon (if desired) in a large, heavy-bottomed pot and turn the heat to medium-high. Cook down, stirring often, for 45 minutes, or until the lemons are very soft. You can add more sugar for a sweeter flavor, but remember that preserves taste sweeter when cool. Check for doneness using a chilled plate (see page 34).

Ladle the marmalade into hot jars, leaving ¼ inch headspace. Check for air bubbles, wipe the rims, and seal. Process for 15 minutes, adjusting for elevation. YIELD: **7 HALF-PINTS**

NOTE: Local honey is more than just delicious—it is also thought to help alleviate seasonal allergies, because it contains pollen from flowers in your area.

Orange blossom water is available at gourmet grocery stores.

Composed of Cara Cara and blood oranges, tangelos, tangerines, and grapefruit, this spread is a citrus-lover's dream.

Citrus Overload Marmalade

2 pounds tangelos
1½ pounds pink (sweet) grapefruit
1 pound blood oranges
2 pounds Cara Cara oranges
1 pound tangerines
3 cups sugar
Zest and juice of 3 lemons
1–3 cups orange juice

Section the tangelos, grapefruit, and blood oranges using a very sharp paring knife (see page 40 for instructions) and place the segments in a large pot.

Cut each of the whole (skin-on) Cara Cara oranges and tangerines into 8 wedges; then cut each piece into ¼- to ⅛-inch slices, being sure to remove any seeds. Place in the pot and add the sugar, zest and juice of 3 lemons, and 3 cups of the orange juice.

Bring to a boil over medium-high heat. Lower the heat to medium and simmer for about 1 hour, stirring often to prevent scorching. If the mixture looks a bit dry (usually due to fruit that's been stored too long), add another cup or so of juice. Test for doneness using a chilled plate (see page 34).

Ladle the marmalade into hot jars, leaving ¼ inch headspace. Check for air bubbles, wipe the rims, and seal. Process for 10 minutes, adjusting for elevation. YIELD: **6 PINTS**

The process of blanching the fruit three times may seem odd, but it's actually standard procedure for candying fruit. Doing so softens the cell walls and allows an even exchange of syrup and water within the fruit. It also removes bitterness from the pith and rind.

Candied Kumquats with Cinnamon and Star Anise

3 pounds kumquats, halved lengthwise
   and seeds removed
2 cups sugar
2 cups water

1 vanilla bean
5 cinnamon sticks
5 star anise pods

Place the kumquats in a large saucepan. Cover with cold water and bring to a boil; then strain and rinse. Repeat this process two more times.

Combine the sugar and water in a medium saucepan and add the seeds scraped from the vanilla bean. Bring to a boil for 2 minutes.

Tightly pack kumquats into hot jars and top with hot syrup, leaving 1/4 inch headspace. Place a cinnamon stick and star anise pod in each jar so they're visible. Check for air bubbles, wipe the rims, and seal. Process for 10 minutes, adjusting for elevation. YIELD: 5 HALF-PINTS

Lemon Ice Cream

4 cups heavy cream
6 large eggs
1 cup fresh lemon juice

2 cups sugar
1 teaspoon vanilla extract
4 tablespoons grated lemon zest, divided

Place the cream in a medium saucepan and simmer over low heat for 7 minutes.

In a medium bowl, whisk the eggs and add the lemon juice, sugar, vanilla, and 2 tablespoons of the zest. Pour the egg mixture into the warm cream and simmer over very low heat, whisking constantly to prevent the egg from cooking. Remove from the heat and strain through a fine-mesh strainer. Cover and chill overnight.

Once the mixture is chilled completely, stir in the remaining 2 tablespoons zest. Process the mixture in an ice-cream maker for 25 to 30 minutes. Freeze the ice cream for at least 6 hours, or until firm. To serve, spoon into bowls and top with candied kumquats. YIELD: 2 QUARTS

Though Meyer lemons are typically used to make preserved lemons, regular lemons work just as well—but look for smaller ones so you can pack more into a jar. The lemons are preserved with their rinds on and need to cure in the jar for about a month. After that, they're supersoft and entirely edible, peel and all. The cured peel is where most of the flavor is. Preserved lemons have a unique taste—tart, salty, and intensely lemony. *—Kelly*

Preserved Lemons

10–12 Meyer or small regular lemons, ends trimmed ¼ inch (see note)
Kosher salt
Fresh lemon juice

Cut a deep X into a trimmed end of each lemon, but don't cut all the way through; leave about ½ inch uncut. The lemon should resemble a four-petal flower. Pack the openings with as much salt as you can. (You can also slice the fruit through and cover with the salt if you prefer smaller pieces, though this may alter the yield.)

Pour 1 tablespoon salt into the bottom of a hot quart jar. Tightly pack with all the lemons, squishing them down to release their juices. Wait a few minutes to make sure enough juice leaches out to cover the fruit. If not, top with more fresh lemon juice. Wipe the rim and secure the lid on the jar.

Leave the jar on a kitchen counter for about a month. Keep adding fresh juice to cover as needed. When the rinds are nice and soft, it's done. Store the jar in the refrigerator, where the lemons will keep for up to a year. YIELD: 1 QUART

NOTE: Preserved lemons are a staple of North African cuisine and are often incorporated into tagines (Moroccan stews) and fish dishes. I frequently use them in my more seasonal "American" dishes, as well. Before using preserved lemons in your cooking, give the fruit a gentle rinse to tone down the salty flavor and slice or dice as needed.

Small, round, yellow Key limes are almost all juice, so they make the best syrup. Key limes are deliciously tart and sweet. They can be difficult to find outside of Florida and well-stocked green markets. If you can't find them, regular limes can be substituted—though regular limes are slightly less tart than Key limes, so you may want to adjust the amount of sugar accordingly.

Ginger Key Lime Syrup

1 pound Key limes, quartered and seeded
1 cup sugar
3 tablespoons finely grated fresh ginger

Place the limes and sugar in a small pot and bring to a boil over medium-high heat. Cook down for about 15 minutes, until the limes release all their juice. Remove the pot from the heat.

Set a strainer over a bowl. Pour the limes into the strainer and allow the juice to drip through. Gently press the pulp with a rubber spatula to extract as much juice as possible. Discard the pulp and peel.

Fold a small piece of cheesecloth in half and place the ginger on top, so that there are two layers of cheesecloth around the ginger. Wrap tightly and squeeze as much ginger juice as possible into the syrup.

Pour the syrup into a large measuring cup. If you have less than 4 cups, add a little water to make up the difference. Pour the syrup back into the pot. Add more sugar if desired, depending on the flavor of your limes. Bring back to a boil so the syrup is nice and hot.

Ladle the syrup into hot jars, leaving ¼ inch headspace. Check for air bubbles, wipe the rims, and seal. Process for 10 minutes, adjusting for elevation.
YIELD: 2 PINTS

Until a few years ago, the sunchoke was called the Jerusalem artichoke, even though it's not native to Jerusalem or related to artichokes. Sunchokes are actually tubers and are part of the sunflower family. This recipe calls for quick pickling—no heat processing required. Slicing the sunchokes very thinly ensures that the herbs and spices adequately permeate the root.

Horseradish Lemon Pepper Sunchokes

2 cups white wine vinegar

2 cups water

2 pounds unpeeled sunchokes, scrubbed and thinly shaved on a mandoline or thinly sliced with a knife

Per jar

4 tablespoons packed finely grated fresh horseradish

3 cloves garlic, peeled

3 lemon slices, ½ inch thick

1 tablespoon black peppercorns

1 teaspoon kosher salt

Bring the vinegar and water to a boil in a small nonreactive pot.

Place horseradish, garlic, lemon, peppercorns, and salt in each hot jar. Tightly pack the jars with sunchokes. Top with boiling brine, making sure the sunchokes are submerged. Secure the jars with lids. Let stand in the refrigerator for a few days before opening. YIELD: 2 QUARTS

NOTE: You could also heat-process these for longer-term storage, though the texture of the sunchokes may be softer. Leave ½ inch headspace, check for air bubbles, wipe the rims, and seal; process in a water bath for 10 minutes, adjusting for elevation.

Sunchokes are easy to grow yourself. Along with asparagus, rhubarb, horseradish, and tomatillos, they're one of the few perennial vegetables. Be sure to keep an eye on them, though, as they do tend to become invasive and can take over your garden bed in a hurry.

Pickling your own garlic means not having to buy fresh bulbs at the market for a long, long time. I end up using Kelly's pickled garlic in pretty much any recipe that calls for garlic—from soups and sauces to roast chicken. I find I use it most frequently when making my homemade vinaigrette. —Jessie

Lemon Herb Pickled Garlic

1 cup white wine vinegar
¼ cup white vinegar
¾ cup water
1 tablespoon kosher salt
1 pound garlic cloves, peeled

Per jar
3 lemon slices
1 rosemary sprig
2 large thyme sprigs
1 tablespoon yellow mustard seed
1 tablespoon brown mustard seed
½ tablespoon chili flakes
1 teaspoon coriander seed
1 teaspoon fennel seed

Bring the vinegars, water, and salt to a boil in a small nonreactive pot. Stir to dissolve the salt.

Place lemon slices, herbs, and spices in each hot jar. Fill the jars with garlic cloves. Pour hot brine over the garlic, leaving ½ inch headspace. Make sure the garlic is covered in liquid. Check for air bubbles, wipe the rims, and seal. Process for 15 minutes, adjusting for elevation. YIELD: **2 PINTS**

Jessie's Homemade Garlic Vinaigrette

⅓ cup olive oil
2 tablespoons pickling brine or white balsamic
    vinegar
Salt and pepper

Pinch of sugar (optional)
Chopped fresh herbs
1–3 cloves Lemon Herb Pickled Garlic

Combine the oil and brine in a reusable dressing container. Season with salt and pepper, sugar, and herbs. Give the container a good shake to emulsify.

Smash the garlic with the broad side of a chef's knife, opening the garlic but keeping the cloves largely intact. Add the garlic to the dressing and shake again. YIELD: ½ **CUP**

TART AND SWEET

Pickled onions are among the most versatile pickles there are. You can chop them up and throw them into soups, salads, and entrées. Their smaller size means you can really amp up the flavor of the pickling brine—and they won't overpower the rest of your recipe. But as the name implies, my favorite way to serve them is to spear a few on a toothpick and add them to a nice cold drink, such as a martini or a Bloody Mary. —Kelly

Pickled Pearl Cocktail Onions

3 cups red wine vinegar
2 cups water
2 tablespoons sugar
2 tablespoons kosher salt
2½ pounds mixed red and white pearl onions, peeled and root ends removed

Per jar
1 clove garlic
2 dill sprigs
1 teaspoon yellow mustard seed
1 teaspoon brown mustard seed
½ teaspoon coriander seed
¼ teaspoon black peppercorns

Bring the vinegar, water, sugar, and salt to a boil in a medium nonreactive pot. Stir to dissolve the sugar and salt.

Place garlic, dill, mustard seeds, coriander, and peppercorns in each hot jar. Pack in the onions tightly. Pour boiling brine over the onions, leaving ½ inch headspace and making sure the onions are covered in liquid.

Check for air bubbles, wipe the rims, and seal. Process for 10 minutes, adjusting for elevation. YIELD: **4 PINTS**

My friend Kai, the consummate herbalist, made this vinegar for me when we lived in northern California. We lived in a small town called Trinidad, in Humboldt County, right off the 101 Highway, which runs up the coast. That area of the country is always damp and cool—and it seemed like those of us who lived there were always coming down with another respiratory infection. Kai's Fire Vinegar is the perfect immunity booster and makes a great gift to bottle up and give to friends when it starts to get chilly outside. —Kelly

Kai's Fire Vinegar

Per jar

2 onions, minced
1½ heads garlic, peeled and minced
½ bunch parsley, finely chopped
1 4" × 2" piece ginger, peeled and chopped
4 jalapeño peppers or to taste, minced
3 bird's-eye chile peppers or to taste, chopped
1–2 thick stalks horseradish, peeled and chopped
A few stalks burdock root, peeled and chopped (optional)
Apple cider vinegar
¼–½ cup honey

Add onions, garlic, parsley, ginger, peppers, horseradish, and burdock root to each jar. Top with the vinegar. Cover and let stand for at least 3 weeks. Strain the vinegar to remove all solids. Add the honey to taste. YIELD: 2 HALF-GALLONS

NOTE: In addition to being a great health tonic, this vinegar blend is also delicious as a salad dressing or poured over roasted veggies.

Spring

On Memorial Day, I like to gather up a few friends and head over to Afton Mountain in Crozet, Virginia, for a day of strawberry picking at Chiles Peach Orchard (they have a strawberry patch, too). I prefer hitting the patch early in the season because I'm not wild about crowds. It can be frustrating to battle fellow pickers for the best, sweetest, juiciest berries. By going a bit early, my friends and I are practically guaranteed to have a good section of the patch all to ourselves (and I get to work on my suntan). I always end up picking between 15 and 20 pounds of the red little hearts and spend the next few days making jars of Kelly's strawberry compotes and preserves. —Jessie

Strawberry Bay Leaf Jam

4 quarts strawberries, hulled and quartered (see page 40)
6–8 fresh bay leaves
Juice of 2 lemons
1½ cups sugar, divided
1 teaspoon calcium water (see page 34)
1 teaspoon Pomona's Universal Pectin powder

Place the strawberries, bay leaves, lemon juice, and 1 cup of the sugar in a large pot over medium-high heat. Bring the mixture to a boil, stirring to facilitate the breakdown of the fruit. Reduce the heat to medium and simmer for 30 to 45 minutes, until the fruit is soft. Stir often to prevent scorching.

Remove from the heat. Pick out the bay leaves and discard. If you prefer a smoother texture, you can blend the mixture in the pot with an immersion blender or in batches in a standing blender or food processor. Return the mixture to the pot and bring it back to a boil. Add the calcium water.

In a small bowl or measuring cup, mix the pectin powder and the remaining ½ cup sugar. Add to the strawberries. Bring everything back to a boil. Skim off any foam. Check for doneness using a chilled plate (see page 34).

Ladle into hot jars, leaving ¼ inch headspace. Check for air bubbles, wipe the rims, and seal. Process for 10 minutes, adjusting for elevation. YIELD: 4 PINTS

Strawberry rhubarb is a classic flavor combination. The sweet juicy straw-berries are complemented by the tart rhubarb. I tend to like mine on the tart side and with chunkier pieces of rhubarb.

This jam is made without pectin so the flavor will be more intense because you are cooking the fruit down for quite a while. The cooking times are approximate and could be slightly longer or shorter depending on the water content of your fruit, so be sure to do the chilled plate test. —Kelly

Strawberry Rhubarb Jam

4 quarts strawberries, hulled and quartered (see page 40)
3½ pounds rhubarb, sliced ¼ inch thick
3 cups sugar
Juice of 2 lemons

Place the strawberries, rhubarb, sugar, and lemon juice in a large pot over medium-high heat and bring to a boil. Lower the heat to medium and simmer for about an hour, stirring frequently to prevent scorching. Skim off any foam. Test for doneness using a chilled plate (see page 34).

Ladle into hot jars, leaving ¼ inch headspace. Check for air bubbles, wipe the rims, and seal. Process for 10 minutes, adjusting for elevation. YIELD: **6 PINTS**

Hearty beet salads have become a mainstay on many restaurant menus. These sweet beets are perfect for making your own beet salad at home. They complement the flavors of sharp arugula, shavings of nutty Parmesan, and earthy walnuts. They're also delicious paired with citrus flavors and blue cheese, as in the recipe on the opposite page.

Sweet Apple Cider Baby Beets

5 pounds baby beets, scrubbed
2 cups apple cider vinegar
1 cup water
2 tablespoons kosher salt
2 tablespoons brown sugar or honey

Per jar
½ teaspoon allspice berries
¼ teaspoon black peppercorns
1 star anise pod
1 cinnamon stick

Trim the beets by cutting off the top part, near the stem, as well as the root "tail." Place the beets in a large nonreactive pot. Cover with water and boil for about 15 minutes, or until the beets are just tender. Strain and run the beets under cold water. Once the beets are cool enough to handle, remove the skins and set the beets aside.

Rinse the pot and bring the vinegar, water, salt, and brown sugar to a boil.

Place allspice, peppercorns, star anise, and cinnamon in each hot jar. Tightly pack beets into the jars without bruising them. Pour boiling brine over the beets, leaving ½ inch headspace. Make sure the beets are fully covered with the liquid.

Check for air bubbles, wipe the rims, and seal. Process for 10 minutes, adjusting for elevation. YIELD: **4 PINTS**

NOTE: The beet skins should slip off easily—just rub them with your fingers. You can wear latex gloves to prevent your fingers from getting stained. If you have trouble slipping off the skins, you can also use a vegetable peeler.

Two Easy Beet Salads for Two

1. Mix 5 or 6 sliced pickled beets, ½ thinly sliced red onion, and about 2 tablespoons chopped fresh dill. Make a dressing by mixing 2 teaspoons freshly grated horseradish and 2 tablespoons crème fraîche. Spoon over the beet mixture.

2. Mix 5 or 6 sliced pickled beets, segments from 3 or 4 fresh Mandarin oranges or clementines, and ½ thinly sliced red onion; place over a bed of watercress. Make a quick dressing by whisking together a few tablespoons of the pickling liquid with a splash of olive or walnut oil. Toss the salad with the dressing. Top with a handful of chopped walnuts and crumbles of a creamy Maytag or Bayley Hazen blue cheese.

Don't limit pickled beets to the pickle plate! Spear a couple of cubes on a toothpick and drop them into your next martini (see page 203). Or use your pickled beets at your next barbecue to make Australian-style hamburgers: Stack a hamburger patty, fried egg, sliced pickled beets, a grilled pineapple ring, and lots of fiery red chili paste between two bun halves. Crazy and delicious!

Pickled Baby Beets with Juniper Berries

5 pounds baby beets, scrubbed (see note)
2 cups champagne vinegar
1 cup water
2 tablespoons kosher salt

Per jar
1 clove garlic
½ teaspoon juniper berries
1 fresh bay leaf
1 star anise pod

Trim the beets by cutting off the top part, near the stem, as well as the root "tail." Place the beets in a large nonreactive pot. Cover with water and boil for about 15 minutes, or until the beets are just tender. Strain and run the beets under cold water. Once the beets are cool enough to handle, remove the skins and set the beets aside.

Rinse the pot and bring the vinegar, water, and salt to a boil.

Place garlic, juniper berries, bay leaf, and star anise in each hot jar. Tightly pack beets into the jars without smashing them. Pour boiling brine over the beets, leaving ½ inch headspace. Make sure the beets are fully covered with the liquid.

Check for air bubbles, wipe the rims, and seal. Process for 10 minutes, adjusting for elevation. YIELD: **4 PINTS**

NOTE: This recipe can also be made with larger beets cut into pieces. Just remember that you will be processing the jars and in turn cooking the beets 10 minutes further in the water bath, so you want to make sure pieces aren't too small, or you'll end up with mushy beets.

This springtime favorite has become quite popular in recent years. One great way to serve pickled asparagus is to chop up the spears for a salad made with farm-fresh hard-boiled eggs, handfuls of chopped watercress, and a bit of homemade mayonnaise. We usually can asparagus in quart jars to preserve as much of the stalk as possible. Whole spears make a perfect garnish for Bloody Marys (see page 202).

Pickled Asparagus

5 cups apple cider vinegar
5 cups rice vinegar
8 cups water
¾ cup kosher salt
7 pounds fresh asparagus, ends trimmed
   (see note)

Per jar

2 cloves garlic, peeled
1 small serrano chile pepper
1 teaspoon black peppercorns
2 teaspoons yellow mustard seed
2 teaspoons brown mustard seed
1 teaspoon coriander seed
1 bay leaf
1 tarragon sprig
1 dill sprig

Bring the vinegars, water, and salt to a boil in a large nonreactive pot. Stir to dissolve the salt.

Place garlic, chile pepper, spices, and herbs in each hot jar. Tightly pack the asparagus vertically in the jars, tips up. Pour boiling liquid over the spears, leaving ½ inch headspace.

Check for air bubbles, wipe the rims, and seal. Process for 10 minutes, adjusting for elevation. Allow the flavors to meld for at least 3 weeks before opening the jars. YIELD: **5 QUARTS**

NOTE: When trimming the bottoms of the asparagus stalks, make sure your spears end up at least an inch shorter than the top of the jar. The tips should not penetrate into the rim area of the jar.

I get my ramps from farmers Jan Greer and Mike Kokas at Paisley Farm in upstate New York. Each spring, they harvest roughly 1,000 pounds of them—quite a feat, as ramps are tricky to cultivate. But their crop continues to expand every year. —*Kelly*

Pickled Ramps

6 cups apple cider or other vinegar (see note)
4 cups water
6 tablespoons kosher salt
6 tablespoons sugar
3 pounds ramps, white bulb and red stem only (see note)

Per jar
1 fresh bay leaf
1 teaspoon brown mustard seed
1 teaspoon yellow mustard seed
½ teaspoon black peppercorns
1 teaspoon coriander seed
1 teaspoon chili flakes

Bring the vinegar, water, salt, and sugar to a boil in a medium nonreactive pot. Stir to dissolve the salt and sugar.

Place a bay leaf and spices in each hot jar. Pack the jars tightly with ramps. Pour boiling brine over the ramps, leaving ½ inch headspace.

Check for air bubbles, wipe the rims, and seal. Process for 10 minutes, adjusting for elevation. YIELD: 4 QUARTS

> NOTE: Don't discard the leafy green ramp tops! Save them for making homemade pesto or Spaghetti with Herby Tomatoes and Brisling Sardines (see page 133).

Ramp Kimchi

5 pounds ramps
3 tablespoons kosher salt
1 tablespoon sugar
1 cup Korean chili powder

3 tablespoons minced fresh ginger
2 tablespoons fish sauce
2 tablespoons minced garlic
1 tablespoon soy sauce

Cut the ramp leaves from the stems and bulbs; remove the roots. Thinly slice the bulbs and stems into rounds; set aside. Mix the ramp leaves, salt, and sugar in a large bowl, and set aside.

In a smaller bowl, mix the sliced ramp bulbs, chili powder, ginger, fish sauce, garlic, and soy sauce to make a paste. Add the paste to the ramp leaves and mix thoroughly. Tightly pack into hot jars and secure with lids. Cure in the refrigerator for at least 2 days. The ramps should be ready in a week's time. YIELD: 2 QUARTS

Sometimes garlic turns blue or green when pickled in vinegar because garlic contains anthocyanins, water-soluble pigments that react under acidic conditions. To prevent this, use mature, cured garlic only. Young garlic is more prone to getting the blues (not to worry—blue garlic is still totally safe to eat). To cure garlic, spread heads on newspapers or wire racks out of direct sunlight in a well-ventilated place for 2 to 3 weeks or until the skins are papery. —Jessie

Five-Spice Chili Soy Pickled Garlic

1½ cups brown rice vinegar
2 tablespoons ume plum vinegar (see note)
½ cup water
1 tablespoon soy sauce
1 pound garlic cloves, peeled

Per jar
1 tablespoon Chinese five-spice powder
1 tablespoon chili flakes

In a small nonreactive saucepan, bring the vinegars, water, and soy sauce to a boil.

Place five-spice powder and chili flakes in each hot jar. Fill the jars with garlic cloves. Pour boiling brine over the garlic, leaving ½ inch headspace. Make sure the garlic is covered in liquid.

Check for air bubbles, wipe the rims, and seal. Process for 15 minutes, adjusting for elevation.

Allow these pickles to sit in a cool, dark place for 2 to 3 weeks before opening.
YIELD: 2 PINTS

NOTE: Ume plum vinegar is made from the juices of pickled ume plums. The taste is quite tart and salty. Ume plum vinegar is available at most Asian food markets, but if you have trouble finding it, you can substitute red wine vinegar.

I think everyone should grow garlic. Just pick up a head of organic garlic at the grocery store and plant the cloves in your garden in early spring. Place the cloves, pointed end up, about an inch or two deep, 4 inches apart. They'll be ready for harvest in the fall, after the tops have died down.

You can make this recipe as a refrigerator pickle or process it. Feel free to use whatever type of mushroom you have available, though refrigerator pickling smaller, more delicate mushrooms like shiitakes, oysters, or enoki will result in a better texture. For larger, thicker varieties such as trumpets, you might want to use heat processing to soften them up. Hot pickled mushrooms are amazing with stir-fries, rice dishes, and soups. —Kelly

Hot Pickled Mushrooms

Enough mushrooms to fill the jars, cleaned and trimmed
3 cups rice vinegar
3 tablespoons ume plum vinegar (see note)
2 cups water
2 tablespoons soy sauce

Per jar
1 tablespoon grated ginger
1 tablespoon minced garlic
1 hot pepper or 1 tablespoon chili flakes (optional)

Before sterilizing the jars, pack them with the cleaned and trimmed mushrooms to get an idea of how many total jars you will need. Empty the jars and sterilize them for canning.

Bring the vinegars, water, and soy sauce to a boil in a medium nonreactive saucepan. Place ginger, garlic, and hot pepper in each hot jar. Carefully pack in the mushrooms.

Refrigerator Pickle Instructions: Pour boiling brine over the packed mushrooms. Wipe the rims and seal. These will keep in the refrigerator for up to 2 months.

Heat Processing Instructions: Pour boiling brine over the packed mushrooms, leaving ½ inch headspace and making sure the mushrooms are submerged. Check for air bubbles, wipe the rims, and seal. Process for 10 minutes, adjusting for elevation. YIELD: 2 TO 4 PINTS (depending on the type of mushrooms used)

NOTE: Ume plum vinegar is made from the juices of pickled ume plums. The taste is quite tart and salty. Ume plum vinegar is available at most Asian food markets, but if you have trouble finding it, you can substitute red wine vinegar.

This recipe may make a bit more brine than you need, depending on the size of your mushrooms.

If you grow garlic, you can grow scapes, which are the flower stems produced by garlic plants before they're fully mature. I love 'em for their brilliant green color and mellow garlic flavor. If you don't grow garlic yourself, the best place to find scapes—which are still somewhat of a specialty item—is at a well-stocked farmers' market. I like sautéing scapes with some shallot and adding them to an omelet or using them as a pickle. This recipe works best with young, tender scapes. —Kelly

Pickled Garlic Scapes

3 cups apple cider vinegar
1 cup water
2 tablespoons kosher salt
4 pounds garlic scapes, cut ends trimmed

Per jar
1 tablespoon minced shallot
1 bay leaf
2 teaspoons brown mustard seed
1 teaspoon yellow mustard seed
1 teaspoon black peppercorns

Bring the vinegar, water, and salt to a boil in a medium nonreactive pot. Stir to dissolve the salt.

Place shallot, bay leaf, mustard seeds, and peppercorns in each hot jar. Pack scapes tightly into the jars. I like to coil them inside the jars for a nicer presentation. Pour boiling brine over the scapes, leaving ½ inch headspace. Make sure the scapes are covered in liquid.

Check for air bubbles, wipe the rims, and seal. Process for 10 minutes, adjusting for elevation. YIELD: **4 PINTS**

NOTE: As with garlic cloves, garlic scapes can take on a blue tint when pickled in vinegar, because the garlic plant contains water-soluble pigment that reacts under acidic conditions. But don't worry—bluish scapes are safe to eat.

Nettles taste a bit like a robust, meatier form of spinach. Here, the nettles are refrigerator pickled (the jars aren't processed in a water bath, which might make the delicate leaves mushy) in a mild cider vinegar that can be incorporated into any savory recipe—rice dishes, salads, soups. This recipe lends itself to different flavor combinations, so feel free to play around with the spice mixture (see the suggestions below).

Pickled Nettles

2½ cups apple cider vinegar (see note)
1½ cups water
3 tablespoons kosher salt
3 tablespoons honey
1½ pounds nettle leaves

Per jar (see note)

2 tablespoons packed finely grated fresh horseradish
2 cloves garlic
1 tablespoon brown mustard seed
1 tablespoon coriander seed
2 teaspoons dill seed
1 teaspoon fennel seed
½ teaspoon celery seed

Bring the vinegar, water, salt, and honey to a boil in a medium nonreactive pot. Stir to dissolve the salt.

Place horseradish, garlic, and spices in each hot jar. Tightly pack in as many nettles as will fit in the jars. Top with boiling brine to wilt the leaves, then pack in the remaining nettles. Wipe the rims and secure with lids. Store the jars in the refrigerator and cure for at least a week before opening. The nettles will be good for a month or so. YIELD: **2 QUARTS**

NOTE: You can replace the apple cider vinegar with white wine vinegar, if you prefer, and add more honey to taste.

You can also try substituting other spices, such as rosemary, thyme, and tarragon.

A single touch of the leaves—which sort of look like basil—brings on an immediate, painful sting. Thankfully, cooking nettles removes the sting from their leaves, making them safe for consumption and canning. But be sure to wear latex gloves while handling nettles and do not rub your face while preparing this recipe!

This refrigerator pickle produces a pretty sharp flavor, but the endive still retains its slightly bitter taste. This recipe is perfect for a pickle plate . . . and superb paired with a creamy, tangy blue cheese or a pungent soft cheese like Camembert. —Kelly

Pickled Endive

3 cups white wine vinegar
2½ cups water
¼ cup sugar
5 heads Belgian endive, outer leaves and root
  end discarded

Per jar
1 large orange slice
2 large thyme sprigs
2 cloves garlic
1 teaspoon black peppercorns

Bring the vinegar, water, and sugar to a boil in a medium nonreactive pot. Stir to dissolve the sugar. Turn off the heat and let the brine sit for 5 minutes while you prepare the rest of the recipe. You want to give the brine a chance to cool somewhat so it doesn't make the leaves too soggy when poured on them.

Place orange, thyme, garlic, and peppercorns in each hot jar. Carefully pack endive leaves into jars as tightly as possible. Top with hot brine. Wipe the rims and seal. Store the cooled jars in the refrigerator, where they will keep for up to 1 month. YIELD: 2 QUARTS

Like morels and wild asparagus, fiddleheads are among the premier forage vegetables of spring. If you're not familiar with them, fiddleheads are the tightly coiled shoots of an ostrich fern plant, and they taste like a cross between asparagus and artichokes. Fiddleheads in their natural state don't exactly look like something you'd *want* to pop into your mouth—but trust me, they are delicious. I like adding chopped pickled fiddleheads to salads, soups, and sandwiches and using them as a substitute for briny olives on homemade pizza. —Jessie

Pickled Fiddleheads

3½ cups white wine vinegar
2½ cups water
2 tablespoons kosher salt
1¾ pounds fiddleheads

Per jar
1 bay leaf
2 cloves garlic
1 tablespoon brown mustard seed
2 teaspoons coriander seed
½ teaspoon black peppercorns
½ teaspoon dill seed
¼ teaspoon celery seed

Bring the vinegar, water, and salt to a boil in a medium nonreactive pot. Stir to dissolve the salt.

Pack the fiddleheads, bay leaf, garlic, and spices into hot jars. Pour boiling brine over the fiddleheads, making sure they're covered in liquid and leaving ½ inch headspace.

Check for air bubbles, wipe the rims, and seal. Process for 10 minutes, adjusting for elevation. YIELD: **4 PINTS**

NOTE: Fiddleheads can taste bitter if not cleaned properly. To prepare, trim the "tail" of the shoot just to where it starts to coil. Soak the heads in cold water and swirl them around, picking and rubbing away any brown flaky bits. Repeat as necessary until all the brown bits have been removed.

Dandelion Salad with Pickled Fiddleheads and Poached Egg

Fill a salad bowl with young dandelion greens (or another bitter green). Add a minced shallot, the zest of ½ lemon, and the juice of the whole lemon. Add a handful of strained pickled fiddleheads. Drizzle with olive oil and season with sea salt and black pepper. Toss and top with a poached egg and a sprinkle of Pecorino cheese. For a more decadent version, add bacon lardons.

Sauerkraut is a type of pickle that isn't canned but fermented. It's really easy to make, though it does require some careful attention. Believe it or not, sauerkraut is made of two ingredients: salt and cabbage. Green cabbage is used to make the kind of kraut you find with bratwurst, but you can use purple, too. If you want to stray from tradition, substitute an equal weight of other veggies, such as thinly sliced brussels sprouts, carrots, onions, or scallions. —*Kelly*

Sauerkraut

5 pounds cabbage, trimmed, cored, and sliced into very thin strips
3 tablespoons kosher salt

Place the cabbage in a 1-gallon stone crock, food-grade plastic bin, or glass container. Add the salt and thoroughly mix the cabbage with your hands or a wooden spoon, tamping down as you go. (The salt will cause the cabbage to release water and create a brine.) Keep packing the cabbage until it's completely submerged in brine. If there isn't enough brine to cover the cabbage, add additional boiled and cooled brine made from 1½ tablespoons kosher salt per 1 quart water. Make sure the cabbage is packed deep enough so that there's at least 4 to 5 inches between it and the top of the container.

Fill a new, clean zip-top bag large enough to fit into the container with water and seal. Place the bag over the cabbage so all the cabbage bits are submerged. Cover the container with a clean dish towel to keep out dust.

Store the container in an out-of-the-way place at room temperature—in the 70° to 75°F range (see note). The kraut will be fully fermented in about 3 to 4 weeks.

I like to start checking and tasting after 2 to 3 days, depending on the temperature of the room. If scum or mold appears on the top or sides of the container, don't worry—that's completely normal. Just skim it off and wash the weighted bag as necessary. The kraut is safe in its briny underwater sanctuary.

When the kraut reaches the desired tangy, sour flavor after the appropriate amount of time has passed, it's done. Skim off any remaining scum.

Ladle the kraut into glass jars, cover it with brine, cap the jars, and store in the fridge for up to 6 months. YIELD: ¾ TO 1 GALLON

NOTE: At a storage temperature of 60° to 65°F, expect the kraut to take 5 to 6 weeks to ferment. At anything over 75°F, kraut may become soft. Anything lower than 60°F and it may not ferment at all.

If you want to can your kraut after it's fully fermented, go right ahead, but know that heat processing kills off the beneficial bacteria created by fermentation. To can, ladle contents and their juices into hot prepared canning jars, leaving ½ inch headspace. Check for air bubbles, wipe rims, and seal. Process for 20 minutes for pints, 25 minutes for quarts.

This is a spicier version of traditional sauerkraut that can be easily adapted to create many different flavor profiles, depending on which spices you choose to use. See the note below for ideas.

Curry Cumin Kraut
(and Other Tasty Kraut Combinations)

5 pounds cabbage, trimmed, cored, and sliced into very thin strips
3 tablespoons kosher salt
3 tablespoons curry powder
3 tablespoons cumin seed

Place the cabbage in a 1-gallon stone crock, food-grade plastic bin, or glass container. Add the salt, curry powder, and cumin and thoroughly mix the cabbage with your hands or a wooden spoon, tamping down as you go. (The salt will cause the cabbage to release water and create a brine.) Keep packing the cabbage until it's completely submerged in brine. If there isn't enough brine to cover the vegetables, add additional boiled and cooled brine made from 1½ tablespoons kosher salt per 1 quart water. Make sure the cabbage is packed deep enough so that there's at least 4 to 5 inches between it and the top of the container.

Fill a new, clean zip-top bag large enough to fit into the container with water and seal. Place the bag over the cabbage so all the cabbage bits are submerged. Cover the container with a clean towel to keep out dust.

Store the container in an out-of-the-way place at room temperature—in the 70° to 75°F range (see note on opposite page). The kraut will be fully fermented in about 3 to 4 weeks.

Check the progress of your kraut every day or two. If scum or mold appears on the top or inside of the container, don't worry—that's completely normal. Just skim it off and wash the weighted bag as necessary. The kraut is safe in its briny underwater sanctuary.

When the kraut reaches the desired tangy, sour flavor after the appropriate amount of time has passed, it's done. Skim off any remaining scum.

Ladle the kraut into glass jars, cover it with brine, cap the jars, and store in the fridge for up to 6 months. YIELD: 3 TO 4 QUARTS

NOTE: Other flavor options:

- Instead of curry and cumin, substitute 1 tablespoon juniper berries.

- Combine 3 minced hot chile peppers, 6 thinly sliced scallions, and 3 cups julienned carrots when adding 5 pounds cabbage to the crock.

I love making kimchi! I usually make a ton of it and dole it out to all my friends. It lasts forever, it's delicious with so many things, and it's good for you as well. This is a basic recipe, but you can make many different kinds of kimchi. There are even delicious recipes out there that use oysters and dried shrimp. If I am feeling under the weather, I would much rather have a kimchi stew than chicken noodle soup. —*Kelly*

Kimchi

2–3 medium Napa cabbages, trimmed, cored, quartered, and sliced into 2-inch-thick ribbons
¼–½ cup kosher salt
2 bunches scallions, thinly sliced
2 cups julienned carrots
A few thick slices galangal, peeled (see note)

1½ cups Korean chili powder
¼ cup fish sauce
¼ cup minced garlic
¼ cup finely grated fresh ginger
2 tablespoons soy sauce

Place the cabbage in a large container or crock and toss with the salt. Cover the cabbage with cool, clean water.

Fill a new, clean zip-top bag large enough to fit into the container with water and seal. Place the bag over the cabbage so all the cabbage bits are submerged. Cover the container with a clean dish towel. Leave out overnight.

The next day, strain the cabbage, reserving the liquid, and place in a large bowl. Add the scallions, carrots, and galangal to the cabbage and mix well.

Mix the chili powder, fish sauce, garlic, ginger, and soy sauce to make a paste. Thoroughly mix the paste into the cabbage and veggies.

Tightly pack the cabbage into quart jars. There should be enough pasty brine to cover the kimchi in each jar.

Cover the jars and allow to sit out at room temperature (between 70° and 75°F). Start checking after a day or two to make sure the kimchi is submerged in brine—if not, it's fine to push it down with your fingertips. Taste it every day. It will be fully fermented in about 3 to 4 weeks. When the kimchi is funky enough for you, stash it in the fridge to stop the fermentation. As long as your kimchi is submerged in brine, it should last quite a long time. YIELD: **ROUGHLY 4 QUARTS**

NOTE: Galangal is a root that looks a lot like ginger and has a sweet, spicy flavor. It and the chili powder are available at most Asian markets.

Summer

Raspberry Jam ◊ Nectarine Orange Blossom Honey Jam ◊ Ginger Cardamom Nectarine Jam ◊ Apricot Jam with Honey ◊ Peach Lavender Jam ◊ Mango Chili Butter ◊ Savory Gooseberry Marmalade ◊ Gooseberry Sauce ◊ Blueberry Lemongrass Syrup ◊ Raspberry Rosewater Syrup ◊ Savory Tart Cherry Preserves ◊ Red Currant Jam ◊ Golden Currant and Star Anise Jam ◊ Blackberry Jam ◊ Blueberry Lemon Honey Jam ◊ Sweet Tart Cherry Compote ◊ Blackberry Syrup ◊ Red Currant Syrup ◊ Canned Whole Berries ◊ Canned Peaches ◊ Canned Plums ◊ Canned Cherries ◊ Plums in Vanilla Syrup ◊ Wasabi Green Beans ◊ Dilly Beans ◊ Mexican Baby Carrots ◊ Pickled Cauliflower ◊ Curry Cauliflower Pickle ◊ Pickled Green Cherry Tomatoes ◊ Soy Garlic Cherry Tomatoes ◊ Curry Carrot Coins ◊ Chili Pickled Okra ◊ Canned Tomatoes ◊ Herby Tomatoes ◊ Tomato Puree ◊ Tomato Sauce with Capers and Olives ◊ Tomato Ketchup ◊ Tangy Orange Tomato Ketchup ◊ Chili Black Pepper Pickled Watermelon ◊ Southeast Asian Carrot Daikon Pickles ◊ Mexican Sour Gherkins with Lemon Verbena ◊ Ginger Garlic Pickles ◊ Spicy Dill Pickles ◊ Soy Garlic Cucumbers ◊ Not-So-Sweet Bread and Butters ◊ Pickled Eggplant ◊ Basil Chili Eggplant ◊ Mexi Bell Peppers ◊ Carrot Jalapeño Relish ◊ Zucchini Relish ◊ Carrot Habanero Hot Sauce ◊ Green Cherry Tomato Chutney ◊ Fire Salsa Verde

The summertime classic! What's better than a generous, gooey smear of raspberry jam on a muffin, biscuit, or piece of toast? This recipe is pretty versatile—it will work for a variety of berries. Try substituting blackberries, boysenberries, dewberries, loganberries, or youngberries if you prefer. —Kelly

Raspberry Jam

3 pounds (10 cups) raspberries
1 tablespoon grated lemon zest
2 teaspoons fresh lemon juice
3 cups sugar, divided
5 teaspoons calcium water (see note)
5 teaspoons Pomona's Universal Pectin powder

Place the berries, lemon zest and juice, and 1½ cups of the sugar in a medium saucepan over medium heat. Stir and mash until mixed well. Once the berries come to a boil, turn the heat to low and simmer for 20 to 30 minutes. Stir occasionally to keep the bottom from burning.

After simmering, you will have approximately 2 quarts (8 cups) of raspberry mixture. Strain half (1 quart or 4 cups) of the berry mixture (see page 41 for instructions), which should yield about 3 cups. Discard the seeds and pulp. Pour the strained berries back into the saucepan with the unstrained berries and add the calcium water. Bring the mixture to a boil.

In a separate bowl, combine the pectin powder and the remaining 1½ cups sugar. Add to the raspberry mixture. Stir to completely dissolve. Return to a boil, stirring often until the jam thickens. Skim off any foam. Test for doneness using a chilled plate (see page 34).

Ladle into hot jars, leaving ¼ inch headspace. Check for air bubbles, wipe the rims, and seal. Process for 10 minutes, adjusting for elevation. YIELD: 5 HALF-PINTS

Nectarines and orange blossom water meld seamlessly with the nuttiness of honey. This jam is a great topper for Belgian waffles, sponge cake, or angel food cake. You can even try a spoonful or two over ice cream.

Nectarine Orange Blossom Honey Jam

4 pounds nectarines, peeled, pitted, and chopped (see page 39)
Juice of 1 lemon
¾ cup honey
½ cup sugar
1½ teaspoons vanilla extract
2½ tablespoons orange blossom water

Bring the nectarines, lemon juice, honey, sugar, and vanilla extract to a boil in a medium pot over medium-high heat. Cook for about 30 minutes, stirring often to prevent sticking, until the fruit is quite broken down. Reduce the heat as necessary.

Remove the pot from the heat and blend in the pot using an immersion blender or transfer in batches to a standing blender or food processor. Blend until smooth. Or, for a chunkier texture, mash with a potato masher. Taste for sweetness. If you decide to add extra sugar or honey, do it by the tablespoon and remember that the jam will taste sweeter when cool. Test for doneness using a chilled plate (see page 34). When the jam mounds up nicely on the plate, add the orange blossom water and stir to mix well.

Ladle into hot jars, leaving ¼ inch headspace. Check for air bubbles, wipe the rims, and seal. Process for 10 minutes, adjusting for elevation. YIELD: 4 PINTS

Cardamom has long been used by herbalists for its warming properties—it's thought to aid in digestion, help with circulation, and calm the nervous system. Whether you're cold or not, a smear of this sweet spiced jam on a piece of toast will warm you right up.

Ginger Cardamom Nectarine Jam

3 pounds nectarines, peeled, pitted, and chopped (see page 39)
1 cup sugar
Juice of 1 lemon
3 tablespoons finely grated fresh ginger
½ teaspoon ground cardamom
¼ teaspoon kosher salt

Bring the nectarines, sugar, lemon juice, ginger, cardamom, and salt to a boil in a medium pot over medium-high heat. Lower the heat slightly and cook down for approximately 30 minutes, stirring often to prevent scorching, until the fruit is quite broken down. Skim off any foam.

Remove the pot from the heat and blend in the pot using an immersion blender or transfer in batches to a standing blender or food processor. Blend until smooth. Or, for a chunkier texture, mash with a potato masher.

Sample for sweetness. You may want to add a touch more sugar, but remember that jam tastes sweeter when cool. Test for doneness using a chilled plate (see page 34).

Ladle into hot jars, leaving ¼ inch headspace. Check for air bubbles, wipe the rims, and seal. Process for 10 minutes, adjusting for elevation. YIELD: 4 PINTS

If you're new to canning, apricots are an ideal fruit to start with. Unlike apples or peaches, apricots don't require any peeling unless you run into a particularly fuzzy batch. (If you do need to peel, see page 39.) In general, though, you can just split them, extract the pit, and throw them into the pot. —Kelly

Apricot Jam with Honey

3 pounds (about 6 cups) fresh apricots, peeled if necessary, pitted, and chopped
¼ cup honey
Juice of 1 lemon
1 cup sugar, divided
6 teaspoons calcium water (see page 34)
4½ teaspoons Pomona's Universal Pectin powder

Bring the apricots, honey, lemon juice, and ½ cup of the sugar to a boil in a medium pot over medium-high heat. Lower the heat to a simmer and simmer for 45 minutes. Remove from the heat and blend in the pot with an immersion blender or transfer in batches to a standing blender or food processor. Blend until smooth. Return the mixture to the pot if necessary and place over medium-high heat. Stir in the calcium water.

In a separate bowl, combine the pectin powder and remaining ½ cup sugar and stir into the apricots. Simmer for another 5 to 10 minutes. Reduce heat if necessary. Test for doneness using a chilled plate (page 34). Apricots will thicken up more than you think, so the freezer test is crucial in this recipe. Skim off any foam.

Ladle into hot jars, leaving ¼ inch headspace. Check for air bubbles, wipe the rims, and seal. Process for 10 minutes, adjusting for elevation. YIELD: 6 HALF-PINTS

The one drawback to apricots is that they can be a little harder to find than other stone fruits because they bruise more easily and generally don't travel well. So if you find a local grower selling these golden fruits, consider yourself lucky and stock up!

This is a very peachy jam with just a hint of lavender. It's perfect for baking and makes a delicious filling for layer cakes, such as the Brown Sugar Cake with Vanilla Buttercream on page 99. Be careful not to overuse the lavender, because it can easily become bitter and too floral. Honey can be substituted for the sugar to give the jam a slightly earthier taste. —Kelly

Peach Lavender Jam

6 pounds peaches, peeled, pitted, and sliced (see page 39)
Juice of 2 lemons
2 cups sugar, divided
6 tablespoons dried lavender flowers
1 cup boiling water
¼ cup calcium water (see page 34)
3 tablespoons Pomona's Universal Pectin powder

Bring the peaches, lemon juice, and 1 cup of the sugar to a boil in a large pot over medium-high heat.

Meanwhile, steep the lavender flowers in the boiling water for 20 minutes. Strain and pour the lavender water over the peaches. Once the fruit has broken down, lower the heat and simmer for 30 minutes.

Remove from the heat and blend in the pot with an immersion blender or transfer in batches to a standing blender or food processor. Blend until smooth. If necessary, return the peach mixture to the pot and bring to a simmer over medium heat. Add the calcium water.

In a separate bowl, combine the pectin powder and the remaining 1 cup sugar. Add this to the peach mixture and simmer for another 20 minutes, or until it has a nice jammy consistency. Check for doneness using a chilled plate (see page 34). You can add more sugar if you like, but the jam will taste sweeter when cool. Skim any foam.

Ladle into hot jars, leaving ¼ inch headspace. Check for air bubbles, wipe the rims, and seal. Process for 10 minutes, adjusting for elevation. YIELD: 5 PINTS

Brown Sugar Cake with Peach Lavender Jam and Vanilla Buttercream

1½ cups all-purpose flour
1½ teaspoons baking powder
½ teaspoon kosher salt
1 stick (8 tablespoons) butter, softened
½ cup packed light brown sugar

2 large eggs
½ cup milk
1 cup Peach Lavender Jam (see page 97), divided
Vanilla Buttercream (recipe follows)

Preheat the oven to 350°F. Line the bottoms of two 6-inch cake pans with parchment paper cut to size and butter the sides and bottoms of the pans generously.

Whisk the flour, baking powder, and salt in a medium bowl. Cream the butter and brown sugar in another bowl with a mixer until fluffy. Add the eggs one at a time. Slowly add the flour, ½ cup at a time, alternating it with a little of the milk until the mixture is combined.

Divide the batter evenly between the cake pans and tap them on the counter to level the batter. Bake for 20 minutes, or until a toothpick inserted in the center comes out clean. Allow to cool for 5 minutes, turn the layers out onto a rack, and cool completely.

Slice each layer in half horizontally, using a long serrated knife, to make a total of 4 layers. Place 1 layer on a cake stand and spread with ⅓ cup of the Peach Lavender Jam. Repeat twice, stacking the layers. Top with the remaining cake layer to build a 4-layer cake. Spread vanilla buttercream on the sides and top of the cake to cover completely.

Vanilla Buttercream

4 large egg whites (½ cup)
1 cup sugar
Pinch of salt

3 sticks (24 tablespoons) unsalted butter, softened
Seeds from 1 vanilla bean

Place the egg whites, sugar, and salt in a medium heatproof mixing bowl over a pan of simmering water and whisk gently and constantly until the egg whites are hot and the sugar is dissolved, about 3 to 4 minutes. Remove from the heat and beat with a mixer until thick, about 5 minutes. Gradually beat in the butter and continue beating until the buttercream is spreadable. Scrape the vanilla seeds (see page 41 for instructions) into the mixture and beat 2 minutes more. Use right away or refrigerate, covered, for up to 5 days.

Mango Chili Butter

4½ pounds ripe mangoes, peeled, pitted, and chopped
    into bite-size pieces
2 cups sugar
3 tablespoons fresh lemon juice
1½ teaspoons ground Aleppo or cayenne pepper

Place the mangoes, sugar, lemon juice, and Aleppo pepper in a wide pot over medium-high heat and bring to a boil. Reduce the heat to medium and cook for 30 to 45 minutes, or until the mango is broken down. Stir often to prevent scorching.

Remove from the heat and blend in the pot with an immersion blender or transfer in batches to a standing blender or food processor. Blend until smooth.

If necessary, return the mixture to the pot. Stir continuously over medium heat until nice and thick. Check for doneness with a chilled spoon (see page 34). Taste for heat and add more pepper if desired.

Ladle into hot jars, leaving ¼ inch headspace. Check for air bubbles, wipe the rims, and seal. Process for 10 minutes, adjusting for elevation. YIELD: 3 PINTS

While gooseberries are relatively uncommon in the United States, the Brits have been jamming and canning this tart green berry for centuries. The cool English summers are particularly well suited for growing them. The berries' astringent tartness is a nice complement to rich proteins, such as mackerel, duck, and goose—which is how the berry got its name. I like to pair the marmalade with cheese and charcuterie. —Kelly

Savory Gooseberry Marmalade

10 cups gooseberries, stems removed
2 thyme sprigs
1 teaspoon black peppercorns
2 allspice berries
1 teaspoon juniper berries
2 strips lemon zest

Place the gooseberries in a large pot. Make a bouquet garni by tying the thyme, peppercorns, allspice, juniper berries, and lemon zest in a piece of cheesecloth (see page 41), add to the pot, and bring to a boil. Reduce the heat to medium-low and simmer for 15 minutes. Gently stir the berries. You want to keep them as whole as possible. Discard the bouquet garni.

Ladle into hot jars, leaving $\frac{1}{4}$ inch headspace. Check for air bubbles, wipe the rims, and seal. Process for 10 minutes, adjusting for elevation. YIELD: 5 HALF-PINTS

Gooseberry Sauce

10 cups gooseberries, stems removed
2 cups sugar

Place the gooseberries and sugar in a large pot and bring to a boil. Reduce the heat to medium-low and simmer for 10 minutes. Gently stir the berries. You want to keep them as whole as possible.

Ladle into hot jars, leaving $\frac{1}{4}$ inch headspace. Check for air bubbles, wipe the rims, and seal. Process for 10 minutes, adjusting for elevation. YIELD: 7 HALF-PINTS

There's a great blueberry patch near Harpers Ferry, West Virginia. The last time I was there, I picked gallons of them. I got home eager to put some up, and I wanted to make something other than blueberry jam. Lemon and blueberries are a classic flavor pairing, and lemons give blueberries a needed boost of acid. For a new twist, I decided to incorporate lemongrass, which lends the syrup an exotic, gingery flavor. —*Kelly*

Blueberry Lemongrass Syrup

6 pints (about 12 cups) blueberries
4 stalks lemongrass, bruised with the back of a chef's knife and chopped (see note)

Grated zest and juice of 2 lemons
2 cups sugar

Combine all ingredients in a large saucepan and bring to a simmer over medium-high heat, stirring often to prevent burning. Lower the heat to a minimum and cook for 30 minutes. Keep stirring every few minutes. When the blueberries have cooked down and the syrup is thick enough to coat the back of a spoon, it is done. Be careful not to overcook the mixture, or it will thicken into a jam. Add more sugar to taste, but keep in mind it will taste sweeter when cool.

> NOTE: To cut lemongrass, trim all but the bottom 3 to 4 inches of the stalks. Discard the tough outer sheath, then bruise and chop the white insides as directed.

Remove from the heat and blend in the pot with an immersion blender or transfer in batches to a standing blender or food processor. Blend until smooth. Strain the liquid through a fine-mesh sieve.

Ladle into hot jars, leaving ¼ inch headspace. Check for air bubbles, wipe the rims, and seal. Process for 10 minutes, adjusting for elevation. YIELD: 4 PINTS

Homemade Yogurt with Blueberry Lemongrass Syrup

1 quart (4 cups) organic whole milk
½ cup organic full-fat plain yogurt

Blueberry Lemongrass Syrup

Preheat the oven to 150°F. Gently heat the milk in a large saucepan until a food-grade thermometer reads 180°F; turn off the heat and allow the milk to cool to 110°F. Stir in the yogurt and pour the contents into a glass or stainless steel bowl with an ovenproof lid. Cover the container and place it in the preheated oven for about 12 hours. (The longer you keep it in, the thicker the consistency).

Place the container in the refrigerator for at least 4 hours, until cold. Once chilled, spoon into serving dishes and drizzle with the syrup. YIELD: 4 SERVINGS

Fresh raspberries are one of summer's sweetest pleasures. But their season is so short, I try to buy them—or pick them, if I'm lucky!—with abandon and preserve them any number of ways, including this syrup that I infuse with a splash of rosewater. My favorite way to enjoy this particular recipe is in a yogurt lassi (see the recipe below) or over coconut ice cream.

—Kelly

Raspberry Rosewater Syrup

2 pounds raspberries
2 cups sugar
3 tablespoons fresh lemon juice
3–4 tablespoons rosewater, to taste (see note)

Place the raspberries, sugar, and lemon juice in a small pot over medium heat. Bring the mixture to a boil and cook for 15 minutes, stirring frequently to prevent scorching. Skim off any foam.

Strain the raspberries (see page 41 for instructions). Return the strained mixture to the pot and bring to a boil over medium heat, stirring frequently. Add rosewater to taste. When the syrup is viscous but still runny, it's done.

Ladle into hot jars, leaving ¼ inch headspace. Check for air bubbles, wipe the rims, and seal. Process for 10 minutes, adjusting for elevation. YIELD: **4 HALF-PINTS**

> NOTE: Rosewater is produced from rose petals that have been distilled in water. It is typically used in cooking to lend a subtle sweetness to desserts and drinks. You can find rosewater at specialty food markets and Middle Eastern or Mediterranean groceries.

Raspberry Rosewater Lassi

In a glass, combine 1 cup plain yogurt and 3 to 4 tablespoons Raspberry Rosewater Syrup. Stir well and serve. If your yogurt is too thick to drink, first dilute it with milk. YIELD: **1 SERVING**

Unlike sweet cherries, sour cherries are soft enough to pit by hand. Just pry them open at the stem with your fingers and gently squeeze out the pit. (For an alternate method, see page 40.) These preserves are an excellent accompaniment to savory meat dishes like pork, game, or turkey. Cherry preserves are also delicious spooned on top of a smear of soft white cheese.

Savory Tart Cherry Preserves

10 pounds (15 cups) tart sour cherries, stemmed and pitted
1 cup sugar
2 tablespoons kosher salt
1 cinnamon stick
1 bay leaf
1 tablespoon black peppercorns
4 whole cloves
1 thyme sprig
1 clove garlic
4 strips lemon zest

Combine the cherries, sugar, and salt in a large pot. Make a bouquet garni by tying the cinnamon stick, bay leaf, peppercorns, cloves, thyme, garlic, and lemon zest in a piece of cheesecloth (see page 41 for instructions). Add to the pot and bring to a boil. Reduce the heat and simmer, stirring often, for 25 to 30 minutes, or until the fruit has broken down and is thick, with enough juice to barely cover the fruit. The finished consistency should be looser than a jam but less dribbly than a syrup. Discard the bouquet garni.

Set a strainer over a bowl. Strain the juice. Set the strained cherries aside. Return the juice to the pot and keep over medium heat, stirring occasionally to prevent sticking.

Divide the strained cherries among hot jars. Ladle hot juice into the jars, leaving ¼ inch headspace. Check for air bubbles, wipe the rims, and seal. Process for 10 minutes, adjusting for elevation. YIELD: **4 PINTS**

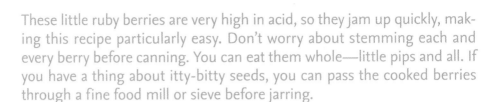

These little ruby berries are very high in acid, so they jam up quickly, making this recipe particularly easy. Don't worry about stemming each and every berry before canning. You can eat them whole—little pips and all. If you have a thing about itty-bitty seeds, you can pass the cooked berries through a fine food mill or sieve before jarring.

Red Currant Jam

7 cups stemmed red currants   1 cup sugar
⅓ cup honey

Place the currants, honey, and sugar in a medium saucepan and bring to a boil over high heat. Reduce the heat and gently boil for 20 minutes, or until very soft. Skim off any foam. Test for doneness using a chilled plate (see page 34).

Ladle into hot jars, leaving ¼ inch headspace. Check for air bubbles, wipe the rims, and seal. Process for 10 minutes, adjusting for elevation. YIELD: **4 HALF-PINTS**

Star anise's pretty, pungent seeds add a warming, licorice-y component to this otherwise simple jam. You can find star anise in the bulk spice section of most natural food stores or Middle Eastern groceries.

Golden Currant and Star Anise Jam

3 pounds golden currants   1 cinnamon stick
2 cups sugar   Juice of 1 lemon
4 star anise pods

Place the currants, sugar, star anise, cinnamon stick, and lemon juice in a medium saucepan and bring to a boil over high heat. Reduce the heat and simmer for 20 to 30 minutes, or until very soft and the berries have broken down. Skim off any foam.

The jam is done when a food-grade thermometer reads 220°F, or when the jam holds its shape on a chilled plate (see page 34). Remove the star anise and cinnamon stick.

Ladle into hot jars, leaving ¼ inch headspace. Check for air bubbles, wipe the rims, and seal. Process for 10 minutes, adjusting for elevation. YIELD: **2 HALF-PINTS**

Blackberries are delicate and very perishable and are best used right away. If you must refrigerate them, lay them in a single layer, covered with a paper towel, and use within 1 or 2 days. Don't wash them until you're ready to use them.

It's nice to try to wait until the dead of winter, when it's cold, dreary, and colorless outside, to break open your first jar of homemade blackberry jam. It's a reminder that winter doesn't last forever.

Blackberry Jam

16 cups blackberries
1 cup sugar
Grated zest and juice of 1 lemon

Place the blackberries, sugar, and lemon zest and juice in a large saucepan and slowly bring to a boil over medium heat, stirring often to prevent scorching. Reduce the heat to medium-low and simmer until the jam looks thick and glossy or until a food-grade thermometer registers 220°F. If you don't have a food thermometer, check for doneness using a chilled plate (see page 34).

Strain half—roughly 8 cups—of the mixture (see page 41 for instructions). Return the strained mixture to the pot with the unstrained berries. Return everything to a boil, stirring often. Turn off the heat.

Ladle into hot jars, leaving $\frac{1}{4}$ inch headspace. Check for air bubbles, wipe the rims, and seal. Process for 10 minutes, adjusting for elevation. YIELD: 7 HALF-PINTS

Once the cherries are pitted, this compote couldn't be easier—just add all the ingredients to a pot and cook down for a half hour or so. If pitting 10 pounds of cherries sounds too daunting, enlist a friend to help. Or feel free to halve the recipe and adjust the yield accordingly.

Sweet Tart Cherry Compote

10 pounds (15 cups) tart sour cherries, stemmed and pitted (see page 40)
1 cup packed light brown sugar
1 cup granulated sugar
1 cinnamon stick
1 tablespoon vanilla extract

Bring the cherries, sugars, cinnamon stick, and vanilla extract to a boil in a large saucepan over medium-high heat. Reduce the heat and allow to simmer for about 25 minutes, or until the juice just barely covers the cherries. The consistency should be viscous but still runny. Remove the cinnamon stick. Skim any foam.

Ladle into hot jars, leaving ¼ inch headspace. Check for air bubbles, wipe the rims, and seal. Process for 10 minutes, adjusting for elevation. YIELD: 4 PINTS

When I lived in Manhattan, going out for cocktails was a weekly—and (ahem) sometimes nightly—occurrence. But since I moved to rural Virginia, my cocktail consumption has taken a nosedive, replaced by my husband's more rustic homebrew. So when Kelly made me her Blackberry Mint Love (see page 203) using luscious blackberry syrup, I felt like I was back in the city. And now that I have four blackberry bushes growing in my backyard, I can easily make Kelly's tasty syrup and libation on my own whenever the mood strikes. —*Jessie*

Blackberry Syrup

6½ pounds (about 24 cups) blackberries
1½ cups sugar
Juice of 1 lemon

Combine the blackberries, sugar, and lemon juice in a large pot and bring to a boil over medium-high heat. Lower the heat to a simmer and cook for 30 minutes. The fruit will break down and the mixture will start to thicken.

When the mixture is thick enough to coat the back of a spoon, strain the seeds by using a food mill or a fine sieve (see page 41 for instructions).

Return the strained mixture to the pot and bring to a boil over medium heat. Reduce the heat to low and simmer until the syrup is viscous but still runny, about 1 minute. Skim any foam.

Ladle into jars, leaving ¼ inch headspace. Check for air bubbles, wipe the rims, and seal. Process for 10 minutes, adjusting for elevation. YIELD: 8 HALF-PINTS

Blackberry Syrup Tea

Stir ¾ cup Blackberry Syrup into a pitcher of unsweetened black tea. Pour over ice and serve.

I really, really love this syrup. It tastes like a SweeTart in a jar. It's great as a cocktail syrup, but I more often add it to mineral water with a squeeze of lime for a simple red currant spritzer. I made this as a small batch because currants can be a little expensive. —Kelly

Red Currant Syrup

4 cups red currants, stemmed
2 cups sugar
Juice of 1 lemon

Combine the currants, sugar, and lemon juice in a small pot and bring to a boil over medium-high heat. Reduce the heat and simmer for 10 to 15 minutes, or until the fruit breaks down and separates from the skin. Strain out the seeds (see page 41 for instructions).

Return the strained mixture to the pot and bring back to a boil. Skim off any foam.

Ladle into hot jars, leaving ¼ inch headspace. Check for air bubbles, wipe the rims, and seal. Process for 10 minutes, adjusting for elevation. YIELD: 2 (12-OUNCE) JARS

In the event you find yourself swimming in berries come summer, putting them up whole means you have the ability to create a bevy of berry-inspired concoctions during the off-season. Crumbles, pies, sauces, smoothies—the sky's the limit. You can use a variety of berries for this recipe: blackberries, blueberries, currants, gooseberries, huckleberries, mulberries, raspberries, loganberries, or currants. A pint of preserved berries in December makes a great gift.

Canned Whole Berries

Simple Syrup (see page 38 and note below)
4–7 pounds ripe berries, caps and stems removed as necessary

Prepare and boil the simple syrup. Place ½ cup hot syrup in each hot jar. Fill the jars with raw berries. Give the jars a gentle shake so the berries settle. Top with more hot syrup, leaving ½ inch headspace.

Check for air bubbles, wipe the rims, and seal. Process for 15 minutes, adjusting for elevation. YIELD: **5 PINTS**

> NOTE: Fruit juice can be substituted for the simple syrup.

Berries with Cookies and Clotted Cream

4–6 shortbread cookies
1 pint Canned Whole Berries, strained
2 teaspoons confectioners' sugar (optional)
Clotted cream or mascarpone

Divide the cookies between 2 small plates. Top each serving with 1 cup berries, 1 teaspoon sugar, and as many heaping tablespoons of cold clotted cream or mascarpone as you require. YIELD: **2 SERVINGS**

A peach is perhaps best enjoyed plain, which is why we've included a basic canning recipe for this favorite summertime fruit. For a spicy variation, consider adding a cinnamon stick, a couple of whole cloves, or a few whole allspice berries—or all three—to each jar.

Canned Peaches

8–12 pounds ripe peaches, blanched and peeled (see page 39)
Anti-browning solution (see page 40)
Simple Syrup (see page 38)

Cut the peeled peaches in half and remove the pits, then soak them in the anti-browning solution.

Meanwhile, prepare the simple syrup in a large saucepan and boil for 5 minutes. Reduce the heat to medium.

Working in batches if necessary, use a slotted spoon to transfer the peaches from the anti-browning solution to the pan of hot syrup. Heat the peaches for no more than 2 minutes (any longer than that and they cook and get mushy), then pack directly into hot jars.

Ladle the hot syrup over the packed peaches until covered, leaving ½ inch headspace. Check for air bubbles, wipe the rims, and seal. Process for 25 minutes, adjusting for elevation. YIELD: 4 QUARTS

NOTE: After you've eaten the peaches, don't pour out the leftover simple syrup! Stash it in the fridge for later use. It'll add a light peachy flavor to cocktails or seltzer. Or you can bring it back to a boil for canning more peaches later.

There are a lot of steps involved in canning peaches. We recommend packing peaches with a friend or two—the time will go by much faster, and you're bound to have a lot more fun.

Purple or prune plums are great for home canning, but you can also use sour damson and greengage as well. You can blanch and peel the plums (for instructions on blanching and preventing browning, see pages 39 and 40), but it's not crucial—plums are often canned whole. If they're very large, halve and pit them first.

Canned Plums

6 pounds ripe plums, stemmed
7 cups Simple Syrup (see page 38)

If canning whole plums, prick the skins in a few places with a fork to prevent splitting.

Boil the simple syrup in a large saucepan for 5 minutes. Reduce the heat to medium.

Working in batches if necessary, add plums to the pan of simple syrup and return to a boil for 2 minutes. Turn off the heat, cover the pan, and let stand for 20 minutes.

Use a slotted spoon to ladle plums into hot jars. Top with hot syrup, leaving ½ inch headspace. Check for air bubbles, wipe the rims, and seal. Process for 15 minutes, adjusting for elevation. YIELD: 5 PINTS

This recipe works for sweet or sour cherries. If using sour cherries, you may want to make a slightly sweeter simple syrup, depending on your preference. (Fruit juice is also a fine substitute for simple syrup.) You have the option of pitting the cherries or leaving them whole, though you'll be able to fit more pitted cherries into jars.

Canned Cherries

Simple Syrup (see page 38)
6 pounds cherries, stemmed and pitted (see page 40)

Prepare the simple syrup and bring to a boil. Pour ½ cup hot syrup into each hot jar. Fill with cherries. Give the jars a gentle shake to settle the cherries. Top with more hot syrup, leaving ½ inch headspace.

Check for air bubbles, wipe the rims, and seal. Process for 25 minutes, adjusting for elevation. YIELD: 5 PINTS

NOTE: If canning unpitted cherries, prick the skins a few times with a clean pin to prevent splitting during processing.

Cherry Lemon Muffins

2 cups all-purpose flour
1 teaspoon baking powder
1 teaspoon baking soda
½ teaspoon salt
½ cup sugar
1 large egg
1 cup yogurt (plain or lemon) or sour cream

5 tablespoons unsalted butter, melted
Grated zest and juice of 1 lemon
1 cup Canned Cherries, strained, pitted, and chopped
Vanilla Buttercream (optional; see page 99)

Preheat the oven to 375°F. Grease a 12-cup muffin pan.

Sift the flour, baking powder, baking soda, salt, and sugar into a large bowl. Lightly beat the egg in a medium bowl and mix in the yogurt, butter, and lemon zest and juice. Add the cherries. Stir the yogurt mixture into the flour mixture until just moistened. Do not overmix. Spoon into the muffin cups.

Bake for 20 minutes, or until a toothpick inserted into the center of a muffin comes out clean. Allow to cool completely. Frost with Vanilla Buttercream, if desired. YIELD: 12 MUFFINS

For this recipe, I like to use small sugar plums or greengage plums. Green-gages are great because they're so high in pectin and flavor. Both types are delicious and quite small, and they don't require any cutting. But go ahead and use a larger variety if that's what you have on hand. Just make sure to halve or quarter them and remove the pits. —Kelly

Plums in Vanilla Syrup

4½ pounds small plums, stemmed
6–8 cups Simple Syrup (see page 38)
2 vanilla beans

Use a paring knife to make a small X incision on the bottom of each plum. This prevents the plums from exploding during processing.

Bring the simple syrup to a boil in a large saucepan. Add the seeds of the scraped vanilla beans (see page 41 for instructions).

Pack the plums into hot jars and cover with the boiling syrup, leaving ½ inch headspace and making sure the plums are fully submerged. Check for air bubbles, wipe the rims, and seal. Process for 25 minutes, adjusting for elevation.
YIELD: **5 PINTS**

I like to use haricot verts in this recipe because they have such a nice flavor and fit well into pint jars. My friend Shawna uses regular green beans but slices them very thinly before packing, so they're more like delicate bean slivers. Regardless of which ones you choose, these beans make a great appetizer. You can adjust the amount of wasabi powder if you like. —Kelly

Wasabi Green Beans

4 cups brown rice vinegar
2 cups water
3 tablespoons kosher salt
4 pounds green beans, trimmed to fit
  into jars

Per jar
1 clove garlic
1 teaspoon finely grated fresh ginger
1 teaspoon soy sauce
2 teaspoons wasabi powder

Bring the vinegar, water, and salt to a boil in a medium nonreactive pot. Stir to dissolve the salt.

Place garlic, ginger, soy sauce, and wasabi powder in each hot jar. Pack the beans in tightly.

Pour boiling brine over the beans, leaving ½ inch headspace and making sure the beans are submerged. Check for air bubbles, wipe the rims, and seal. Process for 10 minutes, adjusting for elevation. YIELD: **4 PINTS**

As the recipe name implies, the herb dill is what makes these beans so "dilly." For the best, most pronounced flavor, we recommend using fresh dill heads—the top of the dill plant after it's gone to seed. But unless you grow the herb yourself, the heads can be hard to come by, which is why dill sprigs are called for here. If you do have access to heads, you'll notice a substantial bump in dilly flavor.

Dilly Beans

4 cups white vinegar
3 tablespoons sherry vinegar
2 cups water
3 tablespoons kosher salt
4 pounds green beans, trimmed to fit into jars

Per jar

3 dill sprigs or 1 dill head
2 cloves garlic
1 teaspoon yellow mustard seed
½ teaspoon brown mustard seed
¼ teaspoon black peppercorns

Bring the vinegars, water, and salt to a boil in a medium nonreactive pot. Stir to dissolve the salt.

Place dill, garlic, mustard seeds, and peppercorns in each hot jar. Pack the beans in tightly.

Pour boiling brine over the beans, leaving ½ inch headspace and making sure the beans are covered in liquid. Check for air bubbles, wipe the rims, and seal. Process for 10 minutes, adjusting for elevation. YIELD: **4 PINTS**

NOTE: Dill is actually a cool-weather plant, so it tends to grow better when planted in the cooler month of April. But for the purpose of making dilly beans, a May planting is fine. If you want, stagger plantings at 2-week intervals from April to May so you have fresh dill all season long. If you don't have a garden, consider planting dill in pots indoors or bringing home a couple of fresh plants from the farmers' market or nursery.

Real baby carrots—slender, immature roots dug up in the early thinning process during cultivation—and dwarf carrots both have a sweeter taste than their fully grown counterparts. Look for them at farmers' markets in the summertime. Windfall Farms in upstate New York sells beautiful orange, purple, and yellow baby carrots that make for very pretty quarts of pickles. Dwarf Thumbelina carrots also work well. —Kelly

Mexican Baby Carrots

5 cups apple cider vinegar
3 cups water
3 tablespoons kosher salt
3 tablespoons brown sugar
4 pounds baby carrots, peeled, topped, and tailed (see note)

Per jar
2 cloves garlic
1 hot pepper, such as habanero
1 cinnamon stick
1 fresh bay leaf
1 tablespoon cumin seed
1 tablespoon coriander seed
1 teaspoon fennel seed
1 teaspoon black peppercorns

Bring the vinegar, water, salt, and brown sugar to a boil in a large nonreactive pot. Stir to dissolve the salt and sugar.

Place garlic, hot pepper, and spices in each hot jar. Pack the jars tightly with baby carrots, being careful not to bruise them.

Pour boiling brine over the carrots, leaving ½ inch headspace and making sure the carrots are covered in liquid. Check for air bubbles, wipe the rims, and seal. Process for 15 minutes, adjusting for elevation. YIELD: 4 QUARTS

NOTE: When prepping the carrots, go ahead and leave ¼ to ½ inch of green stem, but make sure to remove as much grit as possible. This makes for a snazzy presentation.

If, like me, you have been eating fresh tomatoes and herbs all summer long, you may be less inclined to pick your garden clean come late August or early September. But give it one last sweep, because pickling these tasty green fruits is sort of like setting aside a treat for later. If you don't have a garden, your favorite grower at the farmers' market will be more than happy to sell you some green tomatoes before the first frost gets them. —Kelly

Pickled Green Cherry Tomatoes

4 cups white vinegar
2 cups water
¼ cup sugar
2 tablespoons kosher salt
2 quarts green cherry tomatoes

Per jar
2 cloves garlic
1 tablespoon minced shallot
2 dill heads
2 teaspoons yellow mustard seed
1 teaspoon brown mustard seed
1 teaspoon coriander seed
½ teaspoon black peppercorns
¼ teaspoon celery seed

Bring the vinegar, water, sugar, and salt to a boil in a medium nonreactive pot. Stir to dissolve the sugar and salt.

Place garlic, shallot, dill, and spices in each hot jar. Pack jars with tomatoes, being careful not to bruise them.

Pour boiling brine over the tomatoes, leaving ½ inch headspace and making sure the tomatoes are well covered in liquid. Check for air bubbles, wipe the rims, and seal. Process for 10 minutes, adjusting for elevation. YIELD: 6 PINTS

Both cherry tomatoes and dill are relatively easy to grow yourself—even if you have only a window box garden. This is a great recipe to make at the end of the summer, when heat-weary dill is getting ready to go to seed and is full of tiny yellow flowers that offer a superconcentrated hit of flavor.

A quick refrigerator pickle is just the thing when you're not in the mood to process a bunch of jars. For maximum flavor, allow these pickles to cure in the fridge for a week before opening. Mixing red and gold cherry tomatoes makes a really pretty jar. —Kelly

Soy Garlic Cherry Tomatoes

1 cup soy sauce
½ cup rice vinegar
1 tablespoon minced garlic
1 tablespoon finely grated fresh ginger
1 pint cherry tomatoes, halved

Bring the soy sauce and vinegar to a boil. Place the garlic and ginger in a hot jar. Fill with tomato halves and pour hot brine over them, making sure the tomatoes are fully submerged. Wipe the rim and secure with a lid. Cure in the refrigerator for at least 1 week. Once opened, these should last for another week or two. YIELD: 1 QUART

NOTE: While it may seem at odds to pour hot brine over tomatoes destined for the refrigerator, the heat of the vinegar actually blanches the tomatoes a bit, which speeds the curing process.

Pickled carrots are commonly associated with Indian cuisine, which this curry-infused recipe gives nod to. If you want, you can add a hot pepper or a teaspoon of dried chili flakes per jar for a spicier pickle. But let the sealed coins mellow a few weeks before opening so the flavors have a chance to develop fully.

Curry Carrot Coins

3 cups apple cider vinegar
2 cups water
3 tablespoons kosher salt
2¼ pounds carrots, peeled and sliced
    into ¼-inch coins

Per jar
2 cloves garlic
1 fresh bay leaf
1 teaspoon curry powder
1 teaspoon cumin seed
½ teaspoon yellow mustard seed
½ teaspoon coriander
¼ teaspoon black peppercorns

Bring the vinegar, water, and salt to a boil in a medium nonreactive pot. Stir to dissolve the salt.

Place garlic, bay leaf, and spices in each hot jar. Tightly pack in carrot coins. Pour boiling brine over the carrots, leaving ½ inch headspace. Make sure the carrots are covered in liquid.

Check for air bubbles, wipe the rims, and seal. Process for 10 minutes, adjusting for elevation. YIELD: **4 PINTS**

This is one of my most favorite recipes. It's plenty hot, making it a killer addition to nachos (see the recipe below). You can scale back on the spice if you prefer a slightly tamer flavor. When selecting okra, go for pods the diameter of a woman's ring finger. In parts of Asia, okra is actually called "lady fingers" because it's considered the most flavorful at that size. —Kelly

Chili Pickled Okra

4 cups apple cider vinegar
2 cups water
¼ cup sugar
2 tablespoons kosher salt
2 pounds okra, trimmed to fit into jars

Per jar

2 cloves garlic
1 tablespoon minced shallot
1 tablespoon chili flakes
1 tablespoon ground Aleppo or cayenne pepper
1 tablespoon packed finely grated fresh horseradish
½ tablespoon black peppercorns

Bring the vinegar, water, sugar, and salt to a boil in a medium nonreactive pot. Stir to dissolve the sugar and salt.

Place garlic, shallot, chili flakes, and spices in each hot jar. Tightly pack okra into the hot jars without bruising it.

Pour boiling liquid over the okra, leaving ½ inch headspace and making sure the okra is covered in liquid. Check for air bubbles, wipe the rims, and seal. Process for 10 minutes, adjusting for elevation. YIELD: **6 PINTS**

NOTE: Some canners shy away from okra because of the vegetable's inherent gumminess. Okra gum results when the vegetable comes in contact with water or other liquids. As long as you don't cut into okra prior to cooking, gum isn't an issue.

Nachos with Pickled Okra

1 bag corn chips
2–3 cups shredded Monterey Jack cheese
1 small white onion, diced
5–10 Chili Pickled Okra pods, sliced into ¼-inch rounds

Preheat the oven to 350°F. Spread the chips on a baking sheet and sprinkle generously with the cheese. Bake until the cheese is melted, about 10 minutes. Remove from the oven and transfer to a serving platter. Top with onions and okra.

If desired, add sour cream, guacamole, and diced tomatoes, or a few spoonfuls of Carrot Jalapeño Relish (see page 148). YIELD: **4 TO 6 SERVINGS**

We rely on canned tomatoes more than any other preserved food in our pantry, since good tomatoes are hard to find during the off-season. Tomatoes soften during canning, so canned tomatoes are best used for making lovely sauces and tangy soups. Like peaches, tomatoes are typically peeled before canning (see page 39), but it's not imperative.

Canned Tomatoes

12–15 pounds tomatoes, blanched, peeled, and cored
About 8 cups water

Per quart jar

2 tablespoons bottled lemon juice (or 1 tablespoon per pint jar)
1 teaspoon kosher salt (or ½ teaspoon per pint jar)

Leave the tomatoes whole or quarter or halve them, as desired.

Bring the water to a boil in a large saucepan (you may need more or less, depending on the size and cut of the tomatoes). Reduce the heat, but keep the water hot.

Place the appropriate amount of lemon juice and salt in each hot jar. Top with raw tomatoes.

Ladle hot water into the jars to cover the tomatoes, leaving ½ inch headspace. Check for air bubbles, wipe the rims, and seal. Process quarts for 45 minutes, pints for 40 minutes, adjusting for elevation. YIELD: 4 QUARTS OR 8 PINTS

Mom's Tomato Sauce

1 tablespoon olive oil
1 medium onion, chopped
½ green bell pepper, chopped
½ red bell pepper, chopped
3 cloves garlic, sliced or minced
½ pound ground pork sausage (optional)
10 fennel seeds

1 quart Canned Tomatoes, chopped, plus some of the canning juice
3 tablespoons tomato paste
2 tablespoons white wine
1 teaspoon brown sugar
Kosher salt and pepper to taste
3 tablespoons chopped fresh herbs (parsley, oregano, basil)

Heat the oil in a large saucepan over medium heat. Add the onion, peppers, and garlic. Cook until the vegetables are soft, about 6 minutes. Add the pork and cook, breaking up the meat, until it no longer shows pink, about 4 minutes. Strain grease if necessary. Add the fennel, tomatoes and juice, tomato paste, wine, brown sugar, salt, and pepper. Simmer for 15 minutes. Add the herbs and simmer for 15 minutes, adjusting the heat as needed. YIELD: 5 CUPS

This is a more robust version of plain canned tomatoes. I find I go through jars pretty quickly during the winter months, so it's not a bad idea to double or even triple the batch. —Kelly

Herby Tomatoes

2 teaspoons olive oil
5 cloves garlic, crushed
5 pounds tomatoes (plum, Roma, or heirloom), cored and quartered

Herb sprigs (such as basil, dill, oregano, thyme)
Kosher salt and pepper to taste
5 tablespoons bottled lemon juice

Heat the oil in a large pot over medium-high heat. Add the garlic and tomatoes and sauté until soft, about 5 minutes. Add the herbs, salt, and pepper.

Place 1 tablespoon of the lemon juice in each hot jar. Pack the jars tightly with hot tomatoes, leaving ½ inch headspace.

Check for air bubbles, wipe the rims, and seal. Process for 35 minutes, adjusting for elevation. YIELD: 5 PINTS

Tomato puree is the basis for ketchup (see page 134), but it can also be used as the foundation for soups and sauces. This recipe can also be canned on its own. Simply add 2 tablespoons bottled lemon juice per quart jar (or 1 tablespoon per pint) and process in a boiling water bath for 15 minutes. The canning yield for 1 gallon of tomato puree is 4 quarts (or 8 pints).

Tomato Puree

6 pounds tomatoes, cored and quartered

Cook the tomatoes in a large pot over medium heat for 15 minutes, or until the tomatoes are soft. Remove the tomatoes from the heat and, working in batches if necessary, pour them into a strainer set over a large bowl and allow to cool. Transfer the juices that collect in the bowl to another container to be frozen or refrigerated (or used for Bloody Marys). When the tomatoes are cool enough to handle, run them in batches through a food mill or push through a fine strainer set over the bowl to remove the seeds and skins. Discard the seeds and skins. YIELD: 1 GALLON

Feel free to add a few tablespoons of chopped fresh herbs, such as oregano, parsley, or basil, when making this sauce—though I prefer to add herbs when I'm using the sauce, not when canning. —Kelly

Tomato Sauce with Capers and Olives

9 pounds tomatoes, cored and chopped
1 large onion, diced
½ cup minced garlic
1 tablespoon olive oil
2 tablespoons kosher salt

1–2 tablespoons chili flakes
Ground black pepper to taste
¼ cup bottled lemon juice
½ cup capers
½ cup kalamata olives, pitted and halved

Bring the tomatoes to a boil in a large pot over medium-high heat and cook until soft. Remove from the heat. Allow the tomatoes to cool somewhat. Pass them through a food mill to remove the seeds and skins. Set the strained tomatoes aside.

In the same pot, cook the onion, garlic, and oil over low heat until translucent, about 5 minutes. Add the tomatoes, salt, chili flakes, and pepper. Bring the mixture to a boil. Reduce the heat to a simmer and cook down for 20 to 30 minutes, or until it's a sauce consistency. Add the lemon juice, capers, and olives. Season as needed with salt and pepper.

Ladle the sauce into hot jars, leaving ¼ inch headspace. Check for air bubbles, wipe the rims, and seal. Process for 15 minutes, adjusting for elevation. YIELD: **4 PINTS**

Spaghetti with Herby Tomatoes and Brisling Sardines

Heat 2 cups Tomato Sauce with Capers and Olives in a large skillet over medium heat. In a separate pot, cook enough pasta for two servings, stopping 2 minutes before the package directions indicate (see note). Drain, reserving ¼ cup of the boiling water. Add the boiling water to the tomatoes. The starch in the water helps thicken the sauce and gives the pasta something to cling to. Add the drained pasta to the skillet and increase the heat to medium-high. Add ¾ tin of brisling sardines. Toss everything well. Cook 2 minutes more. Divide among two pasta bowls and top each with ¼ cup pecorino cheese.
YIELD: **2 SERVINGS**

NOTE: The pasta finishes cooking in the sauce, so it should still be a little undercooked when you add it to the tomatoes. If you have some leafy green ramp tops on hand, add them when you sauté the tomatoes for extra flavor.

It takes a lot of tomatoes to make a little bit of ketchup, but it's worth the effort. If you end up with more tomato puree than you need, freeze the extra and use it later for soups, sauces, or superfresh Bloody Marys (see page 202). Ketchup math: 1 gallon (16 cups) of tomato puree makes 4 pints of ketchup. —Kelly

Tomato Ketchup

1 gallon (16 cups) Tomato Puree (see page 132)
2 cups minced white onions
5 tablespoons minced garlic
1½ cups white or apple cider vinegar
1 cup sugar
2 tablespoons kosher salt

3 fresh bay leaves
2 tablespoons coriander seed
2 tablespoons yellow mustard seed
2 tablespoons brown mustard seed
2 tablespoons black peppercorns
1 tablespoon allspice berries

Place the tomato puree, onions, garlic, vinegar, sugar, and salt in a large, wide non-reactive pot. Make a bouquet garni by tying the bay leaves and spices in a piece of cheesecloth (see page 41); add to the pot. Cook over medium-high heat until the mixture thickens, about 45 to 60 minutes. Stir frequently to hasten thickening and prevent scorching.

Remove from the heat. Retrieve the bouquet garni, rinse, and set aside. Strain the tomato mixture through a fine-mesh strainer to remove the onions and garlic. Return the mixture to the heat and bring to a boil. Add the bouquet garni back to the pot. Continue to cook down, stirring frequently, until the consistency resembles that of commercial ketchup, anywhere from 20 minutes to an hour. Discard the bouquet garni.

Ladle into hot jars, leaving ¼ inch headspace. Check for air bubbles, wipe the rims, and seal. Process for 15 minutes, adjusting for elevation. Allow to cure for 3 weeks to a month before opening. YIELD: 4 PINTS

Quick Cocktail Sauce

Whisk 1 cup Tomato Ketchup, 3 tablespoons prepared horseradish, 2 tablespoons fresh lemon juice, and a few shakes of Worcestershire sauce in a medium bowl. Serve with steamed shrimp or crab claws.

TART AND SWEET

This recipe was created during a serious canning session with my friend Kathryn, whose garden had yielded an unbelievable number of orange tomatoes. It's a little more involved, as it calls for roasting the tomatoes with a dusting of brown sugar and the cooking time runs into hours, but the zippy caramelized flavor, subtly reminiscent of barbecue sauce, makes it worth it. If you don't have orange tomatoes, substitute red ones. —Jessie

Tangy Orange Tomato Ketchup

12 pounds medium to large orange tomatoes (about 36), cored and quartered
1½ cups + 2 tablespoons packed light brown sugar, divided
1½ cups apple cider vinegar
1 tablespoon kosher salt
1 tablespoon ground black pepper
1 tablespoon curry powder
1 tablespoon turmeric powder
1 tablespoon ground coriander

Preheat the oven to 450°F.

Spread the tomatoes in a single layer on 2 large baking sheets; sprinkle each sheet with 1 tablespoon of the brown sugar. Roast both baking sheets in the oven for 45 minutes, or until the tomatoes brown.

Using a slotted spoon, remove the tomatoes from the baking sheets, leaving behind any juice that collected in the pan. Press the tomatoes through a sieve or run them through a food mill, discarding as many seeds and skins as you can.

Transfer to a large, wide nonreactive pot, add the remaining ingredients, and bring to a boil. Reduce the heat to medium-low and simmer for 3 to 4 hours, or until the mixture has the consistency of commercial ketchup, stirring frequently to hasten thickening. Keep in mind that it will thicken as it cools.

Ladle into hot jars, leaving ¼ inch headspace. Check for air bubbles, wipe the rims, and seal. Process for 15 minutes, adjusting for elevation. YIELD: **7 HALF-PINTS**

TART AND SWEET

This refrigerator pickle is inspired by my friend Dara's first foray to Brighton Beach—a Brooklyn neighborhood largely populated by Russian immigrants—with her fiancé's Russian family. When they walked into a restaurant, Dara was struck by the big, beautiful fruit plates on display. She grabbed a juicy-looking piece of watermelon and took a big bite . . . only to discover that it was a tangy pickle. —Kelly

Chili Black Pepper Pickled Watermelon

½ baby watermelon, washed and quartered
1 cup water
¼ cup white vinegar
½ cup sugar
½ cup kosher salt
2½ tablespoons black peppercorns
1½ tablespoons chili flakes

Leaving the rind on, cut each watermelon quarter into ½-inch-thick wedges. Place the watermelon in an 4-quart or larger glass or plastic container with a lid. Pour in enough cool water to cover the watermelon by about three-quarters.

Heat the water, vinegar, sugar, and salt in a small nonreactive pan. Stir to dissolve the sugar and salt. Stir in the peppercorns and chili flakes.

Add the hot vinegar mixture to the watermelon. Stir to combine and make sure the watermelon is completely covered in liquid. Cover and allow to cure in the refrigerator for 1 week. It's best to eat it (or give it away!) within a week or so. YIELD: 2½ QUARTS

NOTE: It's important to store the watermelon in an 4-quart or larger container. Otherwise the watermelon will taste too salty.

Hot pickled carrot and daikon is a staple of Asian food, particularly Banh Mi, a classic Vietnamese sandwich—it almost doesn't taste right without it. —Kelly

Southeast Asian Carrot Daikon Pickles

3 pounds carrots, peeled and sliced into ¼-inch coins

1 pound daikon, peeled and sliced into ¼-inch coins

¼ cup minced garlic

3 tablespoons minced superhot chile peppers, such as habanero, bird's-eye, Thai, or Scotch bonnet

2 tablespoons finely grated fresh ginger

1 bunch scallions, chopped

3½ cups brown rice vinegar

2½ cups white vinegar

4 cups water

¼ cup sugar

3 tablespoons kosher salt

Place the carrots, daikon, garlic, chile peppers, ginger, and scallions in a large bowl and toss to mix thoroughly.

Bring the vinegars, water, sugar, and salt to a boil in a large nonreactive pot. Stir to dissolve the sugar and salt.

Pack the veggies into hot jars, making sure to get a good proportion of ingredients in each jar. Pour in boiling brine, leaving ½ inch headspace and making sure the veggies are fully covered in liquid.

Check for air bubbles, wipe the rims, and seal. Process for 10 minutes, adjusting for elevation. YIELD: 5 QUARTS

Banh Mi

Banh Mi tends to be heavy on vegetables and lighter on meat, but feel free to play with proportions according to your taste. Vietnamese-style meats can be found at most Asian markets. Most recipes call for using grated carrots and daikon, so you'll want to chop the coins finely before adding to the sandwich.

Cut off a 6-inch section of a fresh, crusty baguette and slice in half horizontally. Onto 1 piece of the baguette, layer 1 slice Vietnamese-style pork (cha lua), 1 slice Vietnamese-style salami, 1 tablespoon thinly sliced bird's-eye chile or jalapeño (or to taste), ½ cup finely chopped Southeast Asian Carrot Daikon Pickles, ¼ cucumber (sliced), and ¼ cup chopped fresh cilantro. On the other half of the baguette, smear a bit of pork liver pâté, hot chili sauce, or both. Combine halves and enjoy. YIELD: 1 SERVING

These newly rediscovered heirloom cucumbers have a very interesting sweet-and-sour flavor. The white flesh tastes sweet, and the skin is surprisingly tart. They can be quite expensive and difficult to find at the farmers' market, but if you grow them yourself or find them growing wild in the South or Southwest, the plants put out a lot of fruit, and they fall from the vine when ripe. They make a perfect garnish for a gin martini. —Kelly

Mexican Sour Gherkins with Lemon Verbena

¼ cup lemon verbena leaves
1 strip lemon zest
¼ teaspoon black peppercorns
4 cups Mexican sour gherkin cucumbers, ends trimmed
1 cup champagne or white wine vinegar
½ cup water
1 teaspoon kosher salt

Place the verbena leaves, lemon zest, and peppercorns in a quart jar. Pack with the cucumbers, being careful not to crush them.

Bring the vinegar, water, and salt to a boil in a small nonreactive pot, stirring to dissolve the salt. Pour over the cucumbers, leaving ½ inch headspace. Make sure the cukes are submerged.

Check for air bubbles, wipe the rim, and seal. Process for 10 minutes, adjusting for elevation. YIELD: 1 QUART

NOTE: Lemon verbena looks similar to Thai basil but is used to add a lemony flavor to food. If you can't find any near you, it's easily available online and is also very easy to grow.

I don't think a sandwich is complete without a few slices of pickle, particularly one of these gingery, garlicky babies. Don't get me wrong—these are divine speared right from the jar, but they're also a major asset to grilled cheese, pulled pork, tuna, Reubens, chicken salad, and of course hamburgers. —Jessie

Ginger Garlic Pickles

4 cups rice vinegar
2 cups water
3 tablespoons kosher salt
6 pounds pickling cucumbers, ends trimmed, quartered into spears (see note)

Per jar
2 tablespoons minced garlic
2 tablespoons finely grated fresh ginger
1 hot pepper, such as habanero or serrano

Bring the vinegar, water, and salt to a boil in a medium nonreactive pot. Stir to dissolve the salt.

Place garlic, ginger, and pepper in each hot jar. Pack cucumbers in as tightly as possible without crushing. Pour in boiling brine, leaving ½ inch headspace. Make sure the cucumbers are submerged in brine.

Check for air bubbles, wipe the rims, and seal. Process for 10 minutes, adjusting for elevation. YIELD: 4 TO 5 QUARTS

NOTE: Because the cucumbers aren't peeled, try to use organic (straight from the garden) cukes. Store-bought varieties are often coated in wax to extend their shelf life. If that's what you're using, make sure to scrub them in hot water first to remove the wax.

This fiery twist on the classic deli spear is perfect for people who love strong flavors and some heat with their pickles.

Spicy Dill Pickles

4 cups white vinegar
2 cups water
¼ cup kosher salt
4½ pounds Kirby cucumbers, ends trimmed, quartered into spears (see note)

Per jar
3 cloves garlic
3 dill heads or 4–5 large dill sprigs
2 hot peppers, such as habanero or serrano
1 tablespoon yellow mustard seed
1 tablespoon brown mustard seed
1 teaspoon dill seed
1 teaspoon black peppercorns

Bring the vinegar, water, and salt to a boil in a medium nonreactive pot. Stir to dissolve the salt.

Place garlic, dill, peppers, and spices in each hot jar. Pack cucumbers in as tightly as possible without crushing. Pour in boiling brine, leaving ½ inch headspace. Make sure the cucumbers are submerged in brine.

Check for air bubbles, wipe the rims, and seal. Process for 15 minutes, adjusting for elevation. YIELD: 4 QUARTS

NOTE: Because the cucumbers aren't peeled, try to use organic (straight from the garden) cukes. Store-bought varieties are often coated in wax to extend their shelf life. If that's what you're using, make sure to scrub them in hot water first to remove the wax.

I'm obsessed with these pickles—they're light and tangy and perfect for serving alongside a meal. Using brown rice vinegar produces a delicate brine that doesn't overwhelm the flavor of the cukes. —Kelly

Soy Garlic Cucumbers

2 cups white vinegar
2 cups brown rice vinegar
3 cups water
⅓ cup soy sauce
6 pounds pickling cucumbers, ends trimmed, sliced into ¼-inch-thick rounds

Per jar

1 tablespoon minced garlic
1 tablespoon minced shallot
1 tablespoon finely grated fresh ginger
1 tablespoon black peppercorns
1 tablespoon chili flakes or 1 hot pepper, such as habanero (optional)

Bring the vinegars, water, and soy sauce to a boil in a medium nonreactive pot.

Place garlic, shallot, ginger, peppercorns, and chili flakes in each hot jar. Pack cucumbers in as tightly as possible without crushing them. Pour in boiling brine, leaving ½ inch headspace. Make sure the cucumbers are submerged in brine.

Check for air bubbles, wipe the rims, and seal. Process for 10 minutes, adjusting for elevation. YIELD: **6 QUARTS**

Some say these pickles were concocted to be eaten with bread and butter; others say the name came about because these pickles are as common as bread and butter. We're not sure which origin sounds more plausible, but we know our interpretation of this canning classic contains approximately seven shovelfuls less sugar than most recipes—you can eat them one after another without going into sugar shock.

Not-So-Sweet Bread and Butters

2 cups apple cider vinegar
2 cups brown rice vinegar
3 cups water
3 cups sugar
⅓ cup kosher salt
6 pounds cucumbers, ends trimmed, sliced into ¼-inch-thick rounds
2 white onions, thinly sliced

Per jar
1 clove garlic
1 tablespoon yellow mustard seed
½ tablespoon brown mustard seed
2 teaspoons chili flakes
½ teaspoon turmeric
¼ teaspoon cayenne pepper
¼ teaspoon celery seed

Bring the vinegars, water, sugar, and salt to a boil in a large nonreactive pot. Stir to dissolve the sugar and salt.

Place garlic and spices in each hot jar. Pack cucumbers and onions in as tightly as possible without crushing. Pour in boiling brine, leaving ½ inch headspace. Make sure the cucumbers and onions are submerged in brine.

Check for air bubbles, wipe the rims, and seal. Process for 10 minutes, adjusting for elevation. YIELD: **6 QUARTS**

When I traveled to Israel a couple of years ago, I ate more eggplant than I thought possible, and I've since gained a deeper appreciation for the aubergine. I like pairing this pickled eggplant with Middle Eastern meze, such as small plates of toasted bread with hummus, lemony cucumber and tomato salad, and olives. —*Jessie*

Pickled Eggplant

1½ cups white vinegar
1½ cups brown rice vinegar
¼ cup packed brown sugar
2 tablespoons kosher salt
2 pounds eggplant, ends removed, cut into
   ½-inch cubes (see note)

Per jar

1 clove garlic
1 hot pepper, such as habanero
1 tablespoon finely grated fresh ginger
1 teaspoon yellow mustard seed
1 tablespoon cumin seed
½ tablespoon coriander seed
½ teaspoon black peppercorns
¼ teaspoon fennel seed

Bring the vinegars, brown sugar, and salt to a boil in a medium nonreactive saucepan. Stir to dissolve the sugar and salt.

Place garlic, hot pepper, and spices in hot jars. Pack eggplant in as tightly as possible without crushing. Pour in boiling brine, leaving ½ inch headspace and making sure the eggplant is covered in liquid.

Check for air bubbles, wipe the rims, and seal. Process for 10 minutes, adjusting for elevation. YIELD: **4 PINTS**

NOTE: Eggplant skin can turn a streaky gray when pickled, so you may want to peel it prior to canning for a more attractive appearance.

Eggplant is wonderful paired with basil, and in a pickle is no exception. You can peel the eggplant or leave the skin on. From a taste perspective, it doesn't matter, though peeled eggplant looks more attractive in the jar.

Basil Chili Eggplant

2 cups white wine vinegar
1 cup water
2 tablespoons kosher salt
2 pounds eggplant, ends removed, cut into
    ½-inch cubes

Per jar
2 cloves garlic
10 fresh basil leaves
2 long strips lemon zest
1 tablespoon chili flakes
½ teaspoon black peppercorns

Bring the vinegar, water, and salt to a boil in a medium nonreactive saucepan. Stir to dissolve the salt.

Place garlic, basil, lemon zest, chili flakes, and peppercorns in hot jars. Pack eggplant in as tightly as possible without crushing. Pour in boiling brine, leaving ½ inch headspace and making sure the eggplant is covered in liquid.

Check for air bubbles, wipe the rims, and seal. Process for 10 minutes, adjusting for elevation. YIELD: **4 PINTS**

TART AND SWEET

Cooks fawn over red bell peppers but are less enthusiastic about their green counterparts, because the concentrated, grassy flavor and astringent skin of green peppers limit their versatility. This recipe is a delicious way to use up the bounty of green bells that many gardeners find themselves overwhelmed by in summer months.

Mexi Bell Peppers

3 cups apple cider vinegar
1½ cups white vinegar
2 cups water
6 tablespoons kosher salt
3 pounds red and/or green bell peppers, sliced
    into ½-inch strips and trimmed to fit the jars

Per jar

2 cloves garlic
1 hot chile pepper, such as jalapeño or habanero
½ cinnamon stick
1 teaspoon cumin seed
½ teaspoon chili flakes
¼ teaspoon black peppercorns

Bring the vinegars, water, and salt to a boil in a medium nonreactive saucepan. Stir to dissolve the salt.

Place garlic, chile pepper, cinnamon stick, cumin, chili flakes, and peppercorns in hot jars. Tightly pack bell pepper strips into each jar. Pour boiling brine over the peppers, leaving ½ inch headspace and making sure the peppers are covered in liquid.

Check for air bubbles, wipe the rims, and seal. Process for 10 minutes, adjusting for elevation. YIELD: 4 PINTS

NOTE: For a great-looking jar that boasts the colors of the Mexican flag, mix green bell peppers with red. Lay the jar on its side when packing in pepper strips and try to keep all strips facing the same direction.

When I first started canning, relish was a mystery to me. I knew it was good for using up surplus produce in my garden, but I could never quite figure out how to eat it. And then one day I finally figured it out: If a dish is boring, add relish. *That's* how you're supposed to approach this condiment—it's an asset to any dish. Kelly's Carrot Jalapeño Relish is incredible on sandwiches or spooned on top of deviled eggs or nachos. —*Jessie*

Carrot Jalapeño Relish

3 pounds carrots, peeled and shredded in a food processor
2 medium red onions, diced
6 jalapeño peppers, seeded and cut into thin strips, roughly the size of the shredded carrots
4 habanero peppers, seeded and cut into thin strips, roughly the size of the jalapeño peppers
6 large cloves garlic, minced

Brine

8 cups apple cider vinegar
4 cups water

6 tablespoons kosher salt
¼ cup packed brown sugar
2 fresh bay leaves

Bouquet garni

2 tablespoons yellow mustard seed
1 tablespoon brown mustard seed
1 tablespoon coriander seed
1 tablespoon black peppercorns
1 cinnamon stick, broken

Mix the carrots, onions, peppers, and garlic in a large bowl.

Place the brine in a large nonreactive saucepan and turn the heat to high.

Make a bouquet garni by tying the mustard seeds, coriander, peppercorns, and cinnamon stick in a piece of cheesecloth (see page 41) and add to the brine. Bring the brine to a boil.

Tightly pack hot jars with the carrot mixture, being careful to get a good mix of everything in each jar.

Remove the bouquet garni from the brine. Pour boiling brine over the vegetables, leaving ½ inch headspace.

Check for air bubbles, wipe the rims, and seal. Process the jars for 10 minutes, adjusting for elevation. YIELD: **7 PINTS**

Gardeners complain of not knowing what to do with all the zucchini their gardens kick out in the summer—especially the kind that seem to grow to the size of your forearm in the span of an afternoon. When I have more zukes than I can handle, I make tons of this spicy relish and give some away to friends. —Kelly

Zucchini Relish

3½ cups apple cider vinegar
1 cup water
1 cup sugar
2 tablespoons kosher salt
3 pounds zucchini, peeled, seeded, and shredded
1 tablespoon yellow mustard seed
1 tablespoon brown mustard seed
1 tablespoon chili flakes
½ tablespoon celery seed

Bring the vinegar, water, sugar, and salt to a boil in a large nonreactive saucepan. Stir to dissolve the sugar and salt.

Add the zucchini, mustard seeds, chili flakes, and celery seed. Reduce the heat and simmer for 7 minutes.

Using a slotted spoon, divide the zucchini among hot jars and top with the remaining liquid, leaving ½ inch headspace.

Check for air bubbles, wipe the rims, and seal. Process for 10 minutes, adjusting for elevation. YIELD: **6 PINTS**

Young, tender, cucumber-size zucchinis are the most flavorful, but if you have some big ones from your garden, go ahead and use them. Just be sure to cut out the mealy, seedy part in the center.

The caramelized sweetness of cooked carrots is a wonderful complement to the citrusy heat of habaneros. This sauce is incredible on everything—eggs, tacos, beans and rice, steamed veggies, and even grilled cheese sandwiches (see the recipe on the opposite page).

Carrot Habanero Hot Sauce

1½ pounds carrots, peeled and sliced into ¼-inch coins
1 large white onion, roughly chopped
1½ cups water
2 tablespoons lemon juice
2 tablespoons kosher salt
3 tablespoons minced garlic

2 tablespoons finely grated fresh ginger
4 habanero peppers, seeded and chopped
2 jalapeño peppers, seeded and chopped
5 cups white vinegar
Grated zest and juice of 1 lime
Ground black pepper to taste

Combine the carrots, onion, water, lemon juice, salt, garlic, and ginger in a medium nonreactive pot over medium-high heat. Cook until the carrots are very soft, about 25 minutes. Add a tablespoon or two of water if the mixture gets too dry.

Once the carrots are soft, add the hot peppers and cook for 5 minutes. Add the vinegar and lime zest and juice. Blend the mixture in the pot with an immersion blender or transfer in batches to a standing blender or food processor. Blend until smooth. Pour into a large container, cover, and refrigerate overnight to let the flavors combine.

The next day, blend the sauce again. Set a fine-mesh strainer over a bowl. Pour the mixture through the strainer, using a rubber spatula to press the liquid through. Discard any remaining chunky bits. (Or, for a chunkier sauce—and bigger yield—forgo straining. Just bring the sauce to a boil.) Wipe off the spatula and scrape the underside of the strainer as well to get every last bit of sauce. Return the sauce to a pot and simmer until it's thick and glossy, about 25 minutes.

Ladle the sauce into hot jars, leaving ¼ inch headspace. Check for air bubbles, wipe the rims, and seal. Process for 10 minutes, adjusting for elevation. YIELD: IF STRAINED, 4 (12-OUNCE) JARS; IF LEFT CHUNKY, 8 JARS

Grilled Cheese Sandwich with Carrot Habanero Hot Sauce

Place 2 or 3 slices of Gruyère or Muenster cheese on a slice of crusty bread. Spread 2 teaspoons Carrot Habanero Hot Sauce (or to taste) on another slice. Make a sandwich.

Melt 1 tablespoon butter in a skillet over medium heat and add the sandwich to the skillet. Cook, gently pressing down with a spatula once or twice, until the bottom is golden brown. Add another tablespoon of butter to the pan, flip the sandwich, and grill until the cheese is completely melted and the other side is golden.

YIELD: 1 SERVING

Green Cherry Tomato Chutney

4 pounds green cherry tomatoes, halved
3 hot chile peppers, seeded and minced
¼ cup minced shallots
2 tablespoons minced garlic
2 tablespoons kosher salt
1 tablespoon finely grated fresh ginger
2 teaspoons brown mustard seed
1½ teaspoons ground dried pepper, such as cayenne or Aleppo
1 teaspoon cumin seed
Juice of 1 lemon

Place the tomatoes, chile peppers, shallots, garlic, salt, ginger, mustard seeds, dried pepper, cumin, and lemon juice in a medium nonreactive pot and bring to a boil over medium-high heat. Reduce the heat and simmer for 15 minutes, or until the tomatoes are completely broken down. The texture should be similar to a marmalade. Season to taste with salt and pepper.

Ladle into hot jars, leaving ½ inch headspace. Check for air bubbles, wipe the rims, and seal. Process for 10 minutes, adjusting for elevation. YIELD: 5 PINTS

If you're concerned about the heat factor in this recipe—it's called fire salsa for a reason—feel free to cut back on the habaneros or substitute a milder chile pepper. And if you want it hotter? Replace some of the jalapeños with more habaneros and be prepared to exhale flames. —Kelly

Fire Salsa Verde

12 Anaheim or other mild peppers
1 large white onion, minced
½ cup bottled lime juice
¼ cup white vinegar
2 tablespoons grated lime zest
6 jalapeño peppers, seeded and minced

2 habanero peppers, seeded and minced
1 bunch scallions, thinly sliced
2 cups chopped fresh cilantro
3 tablespoons minced garlic
3 tablespoons kosher salt
1 teaspoon ground cumin

Heat a large skillet on medium-high until hot. Add the Anaheim peppers (in batches, if necessary) and roast for 2 to 3 minutes per side, or until the skins are charred and blackened. Remove the peppers from the skillet. Once they're cool enough to handle, peel away the charred skins and discard the stems and seeds.

> NOTE: Be sure to wear latex gloves when mincing the peppers.

Place the skinned peppers in a food processor. Add the remaining ingredients. Pulse until the desired consistency. Season with salt to taste.

Ladle the salsa into hot jars, leaving ½ inch headspace. Check for air bubbles, wipe the rims, and seal. Process for 15 minutes, adjusting for elevation. YIELD: 6 HALF-PINTS

When prepping the vegetables, I always chop them to a uniform size even if they're going into a food processor, since the processor can leave big chunks of some stuff and make paste out of the rest. If you start out with everything the same size, you'll achieve a great texture.

Autumn

Concord Grape Jam ◊ Apple Maple Butter ◊ Banana Butter ◊ Banana Vanilla Rum Butter ◊ Pear Butter ◊ Citrus Ginger Pear Butter ◊ Spiced Pear Cardamom Butter ◊ Savory Concord Grape Sauce ◊ Tarted-Up Grapes ◊ Pears Packed in Honey Vanilla Syrup ◊ Chili Pear Fridge Pickle ◊ Pickled Celeriac ◊ Orange Chili Pickled Baby Fennel ◊ Hot 'n' Spicy Pickled Corn ◊ Red Wine Vinegar Onions ◊ Roasted Tomatillo Salsa Verde ◊ Curry Tomatillo Pickles ◊ Pear Chili Chutney ◊ Raisin-Hater's Apple Chutney ◊ Horseradish Beer Mustard

I like using a variety of apples in this recipe—Winesaps, Galas, Honey-crisps, Fujis. An assortment gives the finished butter a really nice blend of tart and sweet. The apples don't need to be perfectly ripe, so this apple butter is a great way to use up less-than-perfect produce. —Kelly

Apple Maple Butter

4 pounds mixed apples, peeled, cored, bruises removed, and cut into ½-inch wedges
1 cup maple sugar
1 cup sugar
1–2 teaspoons ground cinnamon

1 teaspoon grated nutmeg
½ teaspoon kosher salt
¼ teaspoon ground cloves
2 star anise pods
Juice of 1 lemon

Place the apples, sugars, cinnamon, nutmeg, salt, cloves, star anise, and lemon juice in a large heavy-bottomed pot and bring to a simmer over medium-high heat, stirring frequently. Lower the heat a bit and continue to stir. The apples will begin to break down after about 20 minutes, but you can help this process along by mashing with a potato masher or a wooden spoon and stirring often.

After about 1¼ hours, take the pot off the heat and blend the mixture in the pot with an immersion blender or transfer in batches to a standing blender or food processor. Blend until the mixture reaches the desired consistency.

Return the mixture to the pot, if necessary, and cook over medium-low heat for another 20 minutes, or until the butter mounds on a chilled spoon (see page 34) and is thicker than applesauce.

Ladle into hot jars, leaving ¼ inch headspace. Check for air bubbles, wipe the rims, and seal. Process for 15 minutes, adjusting for elevation. YIELD: 4 TO 5 PINTS

Apple Spice Cake

3 cups whole wheat flour
1 teaspoon kosher salt
1 teaspoon baking soda
1 teaspoon ground cinnamon
¼ teaspoon ground cloves
¼ teaspoon ground ginger
½ whole nutmeg, grated

1¼ cups canola oil
2 cups sugar
3 large eggs
2 apples, peeled, cored, and cut into ½-inch dice
1 cup Apple Maple Butter
Demerara or granulated sugar

Preheat the oven to 325°F. Butter and flour a 9-inch round cake pan or Bundt pan (see note).

Whisk the flour, salt, baking soda, cinnamon, cloves, ginger, and nutmeg in a medium bowl to combine. Whisk the oil and sugar in a large bowl; add the eggs 1 at a time and whisk until combined.

In 3 parts, add the dry ingredients to the wet, whisking until smooth. Fold in the apples and apple butter.

Scrape the batter into the prepared pan and sprinkle the top with sugar. Bake for 1 hour 15 minutes, or until a toothpick poked into the center comes out clean. Cool on a rack before removing from the pan.

NOTE: You can substitute cake flour for a lighter, fluffier cake; whole wheat flour produces a slightly denser cake. If you're using a Bundt pan, the baking time and temperature stay the same.

Banana butter is probably the easiest fruit butter to make because unlike other fruits, bananas don't leach juice during cooking and they don't take long to cook down. Light and not too sweet, both of these butters make for a delicious morning spread. —Kelly

Banana Butter

3½ pounds bananas, peeled and chopped
1½ cups packed light brown sugar
¼ cup fresh lemon juice

⅛ teaspoon ground cardamom
⅛ teaspoon ground cinnamon
Pinch of salt

Place the bananas, sugar, lemon juice, cardamom, cinnamon, and salt in a medium pot and cook over medium-high heat for 20 to 30 minutes, stirring often to prevent scorching, until the bananas resemble a thick butter.

Ladle into hot jars, leaving ¼ inch headspace. Check for air bubbles, wipe the rims, and seal. Process for 10 minutes, adjusting for elevation. YIELD: **3 PINTS**

Banana Vanilla Rum Butter

1 vanilla bean
4 pounds bananas, peeled and
   roughly chopped

1½ cups packed light brown sugar
¼ cup fresh lemon juice
½ cup dark rum

Split the vanilla bean and scrape out the seeds (see page 41). Place the seeds and pod in a large, wide pot. Add the bananas, brown sugar, lemon juice, and rum and cook over medium-high heat, stirring frequently, for about 30 minutes, or until the fruit is quite broken down.

Remove from the heat. Discard the vanilla pod. Blend in the pot with an immersion blender or transfer in batches to a standing blender or food processor. Blend until completely smooth. Return the mixture to the pot and cook over low heat until a nice butter consistency is reached.

Ladle into hot jars, leaving ¼ inch headspace. Check for air bubbles, wipe the rims, and seal. Process for 10 minutes, adjusting for elevation. YIELD: **7 HALF-PINTS**

Even though making fruit butter is easy, cooking times vary depending on the water content of the fruit. One of my mom's friends, Tracy, is a long-time canner. She told me that many farmers flood their crops a week before picking, which boosts the crops' weight and makes for bigger fruit. But the extra water content can diminish flavor and add to cooking time. When shopping for pears, know that bigger isn't always better! —Kelly

Pear Butter

6 pounds pears, peeled, cored, and cut into
 ½-inch chunks

1 cup sugar
Juice of 1 large lemon

Place the pears and sugar in a large heavy pot and bring to a simmer over medium-high heat, stirring frequently. Lower the heat and continue to stir. The pears will begin to break down after about 10 minutes, but you can help this process along by mashing with a potato masher or a wooden spoon.

NOTE: You can mix together several different pear varieties for a more pronounced flavor.

After about an hour, remove the pot from the heat and blend in the pot with an immersion blender or transfer in batches to a standing blender or food processor. Blend until smooth.

Return the mixture to the pot, if necessary, and cook over low heat until it reaches a thick consistency. Continue to stir often to prevent scorching. When the butter is nice and thick, test for doneness using a chilled spoon (see page 34). Add lemon juice and stir well to blend.

Ladle into hot jars, leaving ¼ inch headspace. Check for air bubbles, wipe the rims, and seal. Process for 10 minutes, adjusting for elevation. YIELD: 7 PINTS

Buttermilk Biscuits

4 cups all-purpose flour
5 teaspoons baking powder
1 teaspoon baking soda
1 teaspoon kosher salt

1½ sticks (12 tablespoons) cold butter, cut into
 1-inch pieces
1½ cups buttermilk + ¼ cup for brushing
Coarse salt or Demerara sugar for sprinkling

Preheat the oven to 350°F. Line a baking sheet with parchment paper.

NOTE: For a sweeter biscuit, add 2 tablespoons granulated or light brown sugar to the dough.

Whisk the flour, baking powder, baking soda, and salt in a large bowl. Cut in the butter with a pastry blender or 2 knives until the pieces are slightly smaller than pea size. Add 1½ cups buttermilk and mix until the dough just comes together.

Shape the dough into a 1- to 1½-inch-thick pancake. Cut out biscuits with a cutter or a knife. Place on the baking sheet and brush the tops with buttermilk. Sprinkle with salt or sugar.

Bake for 30 to 35 minutes, or until golden brown and you can hear a hollow thump when you tap the bottoms. Serve with pear butter. YIELD: **12 BISCUITS**

Although this recipe may seem like it'll taste ultra-citrusy, the natural sweetness of the pears becomes the dominant flavor as the butter cools. If you prefer a tarter taste, add another couple of oranges or lemons. Bumping up the acidity level is perfectly safe, though you'll have to cook it down longer to achieve a thick buttery consistency. —Jessie

Citrus Ginger Pear Butter

Grated zest and juice of 4 oranges
Grated zest and juice of 3 lemons
3 cups sugar
2 cups water
2 tablespoons finely grated fresh ginger
8 pounds pears, peeled, cored, and roughly chopped
1 cinnamon stick

Place the orange zest and juice, lemon zest and juice, sugar, water, and ginger in a large pot and bring to a boil. Add the pears and cinnamon, reduce the heat to a simmer, and cook for 1½ hours, stirring frequently. When the mixture looks like it's nearing a thick, applesauce consistency, remove the pot from the heat. Discard the cinnamon stick.

Blend in the pot with an immersion blender or transfer in batches to a standing blender or food processor. Blend until smooth. Check for doneness using a chilled plate (see page 34).

Ladle the butter into hot jars, leaving ¼ inch headspace. Check for air bubbles, wipe the rims, and seal. Process for 10 minutes, adjusting for elevation. YIELD: **4 PINTS**

With four pear trees growing in my backyard, I'm always on the hunt for easy canning recipes that use this abundant fruit. Come fall, it's a race to see how quickly I can use up the most pears at a time—and nothing uses up pears faster than pear butter. —Jessie

Spiced Pear Cardamom Butter

6 pounds pears, peeled, cored, and cut into ½-inch chunks
Juice of 1 lemon
1 cup sugar
¼ teaspoon kosher salt
1 teaspoon ground cardamom
1 teaspoon ground ginger
½ teaspoon grated nutmeg
½ teaspoon ground cinnamon
⅛ teaspoon ground cloves

Place the pears, lemon juice, sugar, salt, cardamom, ginger, nutmeg, cinnamon, and cloves in a large heavy pot and bring to a simmer over medium-high heat, stirring frequently. Lower the heat and continue to stir. The pears will begin to break down after about 10 minutes, but you can help this process along by mashing with a potato masher or a wooden spoon.

After about an hour, remove the pot from the heat and blend in the pot with an immersion blender or transfer in batches to a standing blender or food processor. Blend until the mixture reaches the desired consistency.

Return the mixture to the pot, if necessary, and simmer over medium heat for 20 minutes longer, or until the butter mounds on a chilled spoon (see page 34).

Ladle into hot jars, leaving ¼ inch headspace. Check for air bubbles, wipe the rims, and seal. Process for 10 minutes, adjusting for elevation. YIELD: 7 HALF-PINTS

NOTE: Adding a star anise pod or two during cooking also adds a nice flavor. Just be sure to remove them before blending or canning.

Juniper berries, bay leaves, cloves, and star anise bring out a more savory side of grapes, making this sauce perfect for pork tenderloin, duck, or game. I also like eating it with a pungent white cheese like Camembert and crusty bread. —Kelly

Savory Concord Grape Sauce

4½ pounds Concord grapes, stemmed
1 small shallot, sliced into rounds
½ cup sugar
10 juniper berries
2 bay leaves
5 whole cloves
1 star anise pod
¼ teaspoon black peppercorns
Juice of 1 lemon
2 tablespoons white verjuice (see note)

Place the grapes, shallot, sugar, juniper berries, bay leaves, cloves, star anise, peppercorns, and lemon juice in a large pot. Cook over medium-high heat, stirring often, until the grapes are totally broken down, anywhere from 25 to 35 minutes.

Remove the pot from the heat. In small batches, use a rubber spatula to push the mixture through a strainer into a smaller pot, making sure to pass everything through except the skins of the grapes and the spices. It helps to clean off the spatula and then scrape the outside bottom of the strainer so you get all the "meat" of the grape. Discard the grape skins and spices.

Return the strained mixture to the pot and bring back to a boil. Depending on the water content of the grapes, you might want to cook it down a bit more, anywhere from 10 to 30 minutes. Stir in the verjuice.

Ladle into hot jars, leaving ¼ inch headspace. Check for air bubbles, wipe the rims, and seal. Process for 10 minutes, adjusting for elevation. YIELD: 4 PINTS

NOTE: White verjuice is the pressed juice of unripened white grapes (red verjuice is from red grapes). Although tart, verjuice has a softer flavor than vinegar. Its sweet-acidic taste is often used to enhance the flavor of sauces and mustards. Verjuice can be found at finer/gourmet grocery stores and is also available online.

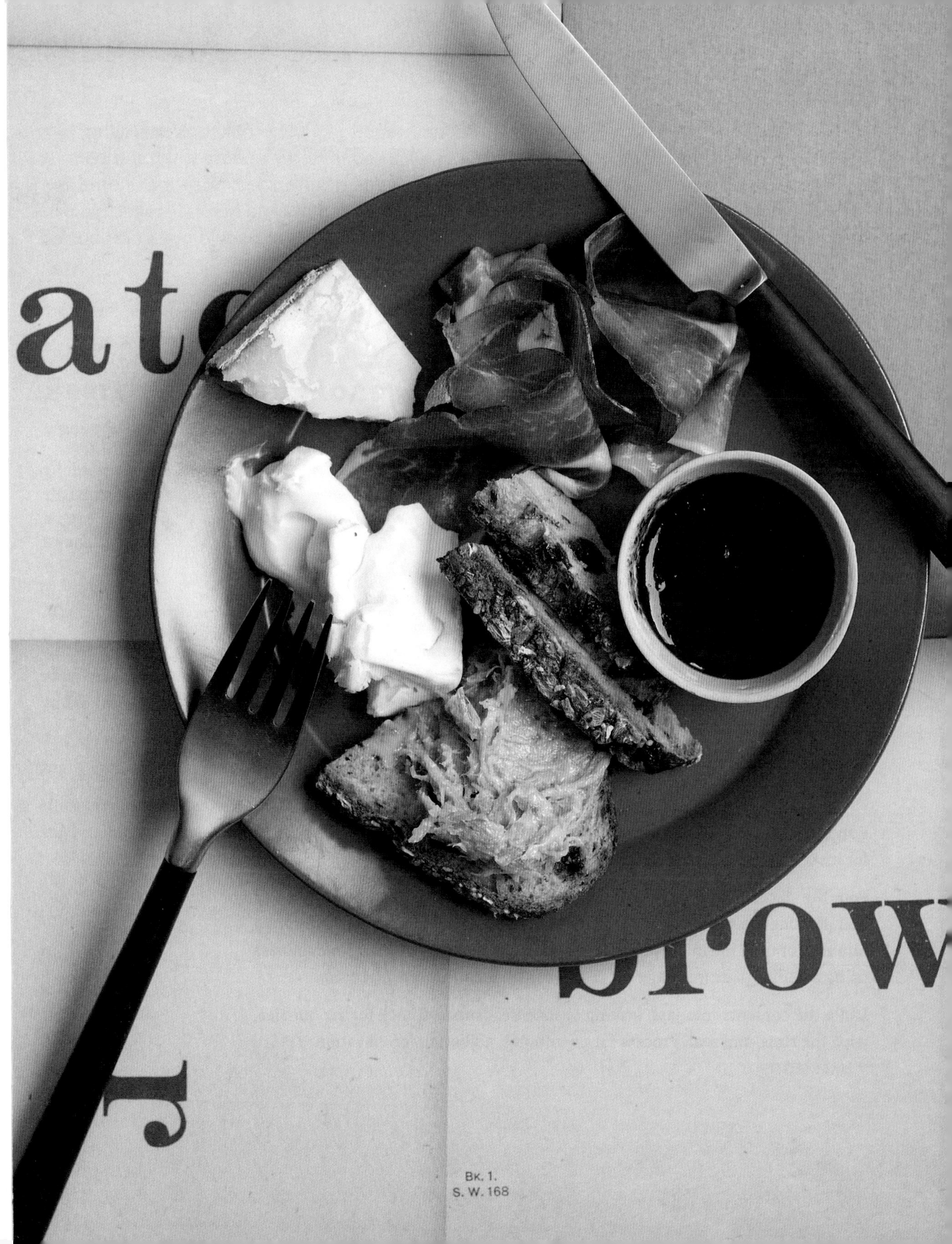
Bk. 1.
S. W. 168

Heat-processing raw pears can make their texture grainy, so I prefer to refrigerator pickle them. They'll keep, refrigerated, for 2 months or so once opened. This recipe works best with pears that are a little underripe, as they stand up to the brine without getting mushy. —Kelly

Chili Pear Fridge Pickles

4 cups apple cider vinegar
2 cups water
¼ cup packed light brown sugar
3 tablespoons kosher salt
2 pounds pears, peeled, quartered, cored,
   and cut into ¼-inch slices

Per jar

1 tablespoon black peppercorns
1 tablespoon chili flakes

Bring the vinegar, water, brown sugar, and salt to a boil in a medium nonreactive pot. Stir to dissolve the sugar and salt.

Place peppercorns and chili flakes in each hot jar. Pack tightly with pear slices. Pour hot brine over the pears, making sure the pears are covered in liquid.

Secure the jars with lids. Allow to cure in the refrigerator for 2 to 3 days before opening them. YIELD: **2 QUARTS**

NOTE: Any pears poking out of the brine will oxidize and turn brown. They're perfectly safe to eat, but they can look a little funny. Make sure the pear slices are fully submerged in the brine before sealing the jars.

This is a very crunchy and refreshing refrigerator pickle. I got the idea for this recipe after trying pickled celeriac on a charcuterie plate at one of my favorite restaurants, Savoy in New York City. It added a nice crunch—a perfect palate cleanser to balance out all the delicious pâtés, rillettes, and cured meats on the plate. —Kelly

Pickled Celeriac

2 cups apple cider vinegar
1½ cups water
1 tablespoon plus 2 teaspoons kosher salt
3 large celeriac roots (about 3 pounds),
   peeled and chopped into 1-inch cubes

Per jar
2 cloves garlic
2 fresh bay leaves
1 tablespoon brown mustard seed
1 teaspoon black peppercorns
1 teaspoon coriander seed

Bring the vinegar, water, and salt to a boil in a medium nonreactive saucepan. Stir to dissolve the salt.

Place garlic, bay leaves, mustard seed, peppercorns, and coriander in each hot jar. Pack celeriac into the jars. Pour in boiling brine. Allow to cool and secure the jars with lids. This pickle will last in the refrigerator about 3 weeks. YIELD: 2 QUARTS

Orange and fennel is a classic flavor pairing, so it stands to reason that the combination also tastes great as a pickle. Here, the fennel is brined in a very light champagne vinegar and accented with chili flakes. I like to eat these as a straight pickle, but they also taste great with triple crème or aged goat cheese. —Kelly

Orange Chili Pickled Baby Fennel

4 pounds baby fennel
6 cups champagne vinegar
4 cups water
5 tablespoons kosher salt

Per jar
¼ teaspoon black peppercorns
1 fresh bay leaf
2 small cloves garlic
½ teaspoon chili flakes or ½ teaspoon coriander seed
3 strips orange zest

Trim the stalks and fronds from the fennel, leaving only the bulbs. Halve or quarter the bulbs so they're about an inch in diameter.

Bring the vinegar, water, and salt to a boil in a medium nonreactive pot. Stir to dissolve the salt.

Place peppercorns, bay leaf, garlic, chili flakes, and orange zest in each hot jar. Tightly pack fennel into the jars. Pour in boiling brine, leaving ½ inch headspace.

Check for air bubbles, wipe the rims, and seal. Process for 10 minutes, adjusting for elevation. YIELD: **8 PINTS**

There's nothing better than fresh corn! Well, except for pickled corn with chili flakes. Add to a quesadilla, tacos, or nachos.

Hot 'n' Spicy Pickled Corn

8 cups sweet corn (shaved from roughly 14–16 ears)
1 large white onion, minced
3 cups white vinegar
1 cup water
3 tablespoons sugar
3 tablespoons kosher salt

Per jar
1 tablespoon minced garlic
2 habanero peppers
1 tablespoon chili flakes
1 tablespoon brown mustard seed

Mix the corn and onion in a large bowl. Bring the vinegar, water, sugar, and salt to a boil in a medium nonreactive pot. Stir to dissolve the sugar and salt.

Place garlic, peppers, chili flakes, and mustard seed in each hot jar. Pack with the corn mixture. Pour boiling brine into the jars, leaving ½ inch headspace and making sure the corn is submerged.

Check for air bubbles, wipe the rims, and seal. Process for 10 minutes, adjusting for elevation. YIELD: 5 PINTS

These pickled onions are great on top of a burger, with braised beef short ribs or pork, with a poached egg, or on almost any sandwich! —Kelly

Red Wine Vinegar Onions

3 cups red wine vinegar
1 cup water
1 tablespoon sugar
1 tablespoon kosher salt
3 large red onions, sliced ¼ inch thick (see note on the opposite page)

Per jar
2 cloves garlic
1 fresh bay leaf
1 tablespoon yellow mustard seed
1 tablespoon brown mustard seed
1 tablespoon black peppercorns

Bring the vinegar, water, sugar, and salt to a boil in a medium nonreactive pot. Stir to dissolve the sugar and salt.

NOTE: Depending on the size of your onions, you may need more to fill up each quart jar.

Place garlic, bay leaf, mustard seeds, and peppercorns in each hot jar. Pack tightly with onion rings. Pour boiling brine over the onions, leaving ½ inch headspace and making sure onions are submerged.

Check for air bubbles, wipe the rims, and seal. Process for 10 minutes, adjusting for elevation. YIELD: 2 QUARTS

Braised Beef Short Ribs with Pickled Onions

8 short ribs
Kosher salt and pepper
¼ cup canola oil
1 large white onion, roughly chopped
1 head garlic, separated into cloves, peeled, and crushed
3 stalks celery, cut into 2-inch chunks

2 carrots, peeled and roughly chopped
2 tablespoons tomato paste
2 fresh bay leaves
2 large thyme sprigs
1–3 bottles dry red wine (see note)
2–3 quarts beef stock
Red Wine Vinegar Onions

Preheat the oven to 350°F. Pat the ribs dry with a paper towel and season generously with salt and pepper.

NOTE: You can make this recipe with one bottle of wine—or two or three and reduce it down until you have roughly 4 cups' worth for a super-rich sauce. If you choose to go with multiple bottles of wine, reduce it before you begin.

Heat the oil in a Dutch oven on high until quite hot. Working 4 at a time, brown the ribs until there's a nice crust all the way around; set aside. Add the onion, garlic, celery, and carrots to the pot and cook for about 10 minutes. Add the tomato paste, bay leaves, and thyme; mix well. Pour in the wine. Add the ribs and enough beef stock to just cover everything.

Cover the pot and bake for 1½ hours. After that, begin checking the meat every 30 minutes. It should be quite tender and falling off the bone. I always sample a little piece, since the meat may look done but may still be a bit chewy. The meat can take up to 3 hours to cook, depending on the cut and quality of the ribs.

When the meat is fully tender, remove it from the oven and allow to cool in the pot (which may take overnight; refrigerate). Remove the ribs and set aside. Bring the remaining liquid in the pot to a simmer and reduce to about 4 cups, which can take anywhere from 20 minutes to an hour. Skim off any fat as you go.

Taste the sauce. It may be quite rich at this point. If so, stop now and strain out the solids through a fine-mesh strainer. For a richer sauce, keep reducing and tasting until you are happy with the flavor. When you are ready to serve, heat the ribs in a dish in the oven at 350°F and serve with sauce drizzled over. Top with the onions. YIELD: 4 SERVINGS

Leaving on the charred tomatillo skins after broiling gives the salsa added flavor. If you want, you can dial down the heat by using fewer habaneros or by substituting milder peppers, like pasillas. —Kelly

Roasted Tomatillo Salsa Verde

5 pounds tomatillos, husked and halved
2 small onions, chopped
1½ tablespoons chopped garlic
1½ tablespoons kosher salt
3 habanero chile peppers, seeded and chopped

2 Anaheim chile peppers, seeded and chopped
2 pasilla chile peppers, seeded and chopped
2 tablespoons chopped fresh cilantro
Grated zest and juice of 1 lime

Place the tomatillos cut side down on a baking sheet and set 4 inches below a very hot broiler. Once charred, flip and roast on the other side. Allow to cool.

Transfer the charred tomatillos plus their collected juices to a food processor. Add the onions, garlic, salt, chile peppers, cilantro, and lime. Pulse.

Pour into a large saucepan and bring to a boil, stirring frequently to prevent burning. Reduce the heat to low and simmer for 10 minutes.

Ladle into jars, leaving ½ inch headspace. Check for air bubbles, wipe the rims, and seal. Process for 15 minutes, adjusting for elevation. YIELD: **3 PINTS**

> NOTE: Store fresh tomatillos with husks in a paper bag in the refrigerator for 2 weeks. For longer storage, remove the husks; they'll keep in the refrigerator for up to 3 months.

Pan-Roasted Chicken with Salsa Verde

1 whole chicken, cut into serving pieces
Kosher salt and pepper
3 tablespoons canola oil

Butter
3 tablespoons lime juice
Roasted Tomatillo Salsa Verde

Preheat the oven to 425°F. Salt and pepper the chicken. Heat the oil in a large oven-proof skillet over high heat. Add the chicken, skin side down, and cook until golden on the bottom; flip the pieces. Place a pat of butter on top of each piece.

Transfer the skillet to the oven for 10 minutes, then return to the burner over high heat. Melt a few tablespoons of butter in the pan; add the lime juice. Spoon butter sauce over each piece of chicken several times.

Place the chicken back in the oven for 15 minutes, or until the juices run clear when the meat is sliced. Remove from the oven and let the chicken rest for 5 minutes. Serve topped with the salsa verde. YIELD: **4 SERVINGS**

When I was sous-chef at a restaurant in downtown Manhattan, we made a similar pickle to go with pork butt braised in apple cider with curry. I really liked to play around with that recipe, and this is my version. —*Kelly*

Curry Tomatillo Pickles

3 cups apple cider vinegar
2 cups brown rice vinegar
3 cups water
½ cup packed light brown sugar
⅓ cup curry powder
¼ cup kosher salt
5 pounds tomatillos, husked and quartered

Per jar

1 clove garlic
1 tablespoon chopped onion or shallot
½ tablespoon yellow mustard seed
½ tablespoon brown mustard seed
¼ teaspoon black peppercorns
¼ teaspoon cayenne or aleppo pepper

Bring the vinegars, water, brown sugar, curry powder, and salt to a boil in a large nonreactive pot.

Place garlic, onion, mustard seeds, peppercorns, and cayenne pepper in each hot jar. Pack the jars tightly with tomatillos. Pour in boiling brine, leaving ½ inch headspace.

Check for air bubbles, wipe the rims, and seal. Process for 10 minutes, adjusting for elevation. Store the jars in a cool, dark place for 2 to 3 weeks before opening. YIELD: 5 QUARTS

NOTE: For more flavor, add ¼ teaspoon coriander or additional curry powder to each jar. If you want a hotter pickle, you can also add a hot chile pepper to each jar.

This recipe is adapted from one developed by my mom's friend Tracy, who's a big-time canner. It was inspired by a cooking class she took in Morocco, an experience that she says greatly expanded her spice repertoire. Since then, she's been incorporating more cardamom, cumin, dry mustard, and Indian ghee into her cooking. This deliciously balanced chutney is no exception. —Kelly

Pear Chili Chutney

3 pounds pears, peeled, cored, and chopped
3 tablespoons lemon juice
1 teaspoon ghee (see note)
1 large onion, diced
2 tablespoons minced garlic
2½ tablespoons finely grated fresh ginger
½ tablespoon chili flakes
½ tablespoon dry mustard
1 tablespoon cayenne or Aleppo pepper

1 cup malt vinegar
1 cup packed light brown sugar
2 tablespoons kosher salt
3 fresh bay leaves
1½ tablespoons allspice berries
2 teaspoons cardamom seed
½ tablespoon coriander seed
¼ teaspoon whole cloves

Mix the pears with the lemon juice in a large bowl to keep them from browning.

Combine the ghee, onion, garlic, ginger, chili flakes, mustard, and cayenne pepper in a large nonreactive pot over low heat. Cook, stirring often, until the onions are translucent, 5 to 7 minutes. Add the pears and mix well.

Increase the heat to medium. Add the vinegar, brown sugar, and salt. Make a bouquet garni by tying the bay leaves, allspice, cardamom, coriander, and cloves in a piece of cheesecloth (see page 41) and add to the pot.

Cook for 45 to 60 minutes, depending on the water content of the fruit. As the pears break down, stir often to prevent scorching.

Check for doneness by dragging a spoon across the bottom of the pot. If the mixture parts for a moment, it's ready. Season with salt and discard the bouquet garni.

Ladle into hot jars, leaving ¼ inch headspace. Check for air bubbles, wipe the rims, and seal. Process for 10 minutes, adjusting for elevation. YIELD: 5 HALF-PINTS

NOTE: Ghee is Indian clarified (concentrated) butter. It's available at well-stocked grocery stores and ethnic markets.

I call this Raisin-Hater's Apple Chutney because I'm not usually a fan of mixing raisins with savory flavors. When testing this recipe, the other cooks in my kitchen winced when they saw this ingredient. "Raisins?" they asked, concerned. But after tasting it, even raisin haters were converted. This chutney is delicious with everything from naan to roast pork. —Kelly

Raisin-Hater's Apple Chutney

3 pounds apples, cored, peeled, and chopped into ½-inch cubes
3 tablespoons fresh lemon juice
1 teaspoon ghee or canola oil (see note)
1 large white onion, minced
2 tablespoons ground cumin
2 tablespoons kosher salt
1 tablespoon yellow mustard seed
1 tablespoon chili flakes
1 tablespoon ground ginger
1 cup packed light brown sugar
1 cup apple cider vinegar
1 cup raisins, preferably flame
Kosher salt and pepper to taste

Mix the apples with the lemon juice in a large bowl to keep them from browning.

Combine the ghee, onion, cumin, salt, mustard seed, chili flakes, and ginger in a medium nonreactive pot over low heat. Cook and stir often until the onions are translucent, about 5 to 7 minutes. Add the apples and mix well.

Increase the heat to medium. Add the brown sugar and vinegar. Cook for about 30 minutes. Add the raisins and cook for another 15 minutes or so, stirring frequently, until the mixture has a thick consistency. Season with salt and pepper.

Ladle into hot jars, leaving ½ inch headspace. Check for air bubbles, wipe the rims, and seal. Process for 10 minutes, adjusting for elevation. YIELD: 5 PINTS

NOTE: Naan is a type of leavened Indian flatbread. It comes in many varieties and can usually be found at larger supermarkets or at your local specialty foods store.

This recipe is a great way to take advantage of fresh horseradish root in the fall. But be forewarned—this mustard is really hot and pungent when you first make it. The flavors will mellow after a while. I like to use Coleman's dry mustard. Adding a splash of dark beer makes this a great dip for sausages—and perfect for Oktoberfest. —*Kelly*

Horseradish Beer Mustard

½ cup dry mustard
½ cup dark beer
½ cup finely grated fresh horseradish (see note)
1 tablespoon brown mustard seed
Kosher salt and pepper to taste

Whisk the dry mustard, beer, horseradish, mustard seed, salt, and pepper in a bowl to blend. Cover and refrigerate overnight to allow the flavors to meld and mellow. Keep chilled.

For canning, add ¾ teaspoon white vinegar to the mixture, then ladle into hot jars, leaving ¼ inch headspace. Check for air bubbles, wipe the rims, and seal. Process for 10 minutes, adjusting for elevation. YIELD: 3 (4-OUNCE) JARS

NOTE: When fresh horseradish is grated (as opposed to chopped or sliced), its pungent oils are released, which brings out the root's natural bite. But be cautious when grating, since the oils released into the air can make your eyes and nose burn.

I generally prefer not to heat-process this recipe, since horseradish loses flavor as it cooks. If you do want to can it for long-term storage, add a little bit of vinegar to the mixture before jarring to help stabilize the flavor of the horseradish.

IDEAS AND SOLUTIONS

Can Jam:
Can, Drink,
and Be
Merry

Canning isn't meant to be a solo affair—you know this is true if you've ever hulled a flat of strawberries or chopped a mountain of tomatoes by yourself. Back in the day, when it was common for families to put up 500 to 600 jars of seasonal produce for the winter, people would bring their own fruits and vegetables to community canneries—facilities with large-scale kitchens—where neighbors would gather to process piles of food together. The workload was spread around evenly, making the process that much faster (and more enjoyable). Community canneries have been making quite a comeback in recent years, but you can easily replicate the experience by hosting a canning party at home.

How it works: Invite over a group of friends. Decide what you want to can (one or two recipes, at most) and ask everyone to bring a portion of the ingredients, equipment, and jars. Assign each guest a specific task—a couple of people can prep and chop the produce, another might scald the jars, another packs the jars, etc. Experienced canners can share tips and advice. Beginners get to learn the craft. Everyone hangs out, chats, laughs, and sips a cocktail or two. But unlike a regular cocktail party, there's a sense of accomplishment and purpose at the end: You worked hard for every delicious quart of tomatoes.

There is also a bit of Tom Sawyer–ism involved in hosting a canning party; while your guests may be excited to come over and eat, drink, and be merry, some—particularly canning neophytes—may be surprised to find that they are expected to peel and core 20 pounds of apples. So the first rule of hosting a preserving party is: Only invite people who *want* to can. The second rule is: Make it a good time. We've been to and hosted quite a few canning parties, and we think the best ones—those that become annual events that guests look forward to each year—are the ones that don't short-shrift fun. Good food, drinks, the right music, even lighthearted party themes are a great way to foster that festive communal atmosphere you're after. We've put together some suggestions for throwing a successful canning party that your friends and neighbors will still be talking about next year.

BEFORE THE PARTY: MAKE A PLAN

FIGURE OUT WHAT TO CAN, THEN COME UP WITH THE GUEST LIST. It's no fun for some guests to stand around twiddling their thumbs while others are busy making jams and pickles, so figure out how many people you'll need to make the recipe (and yield) you want. Three to six guests is a good number, depending on the size of your kitchen. It's always a good idea to include at least one other seasoned canner on the guest list.

DECIDE: JAMS OR PICKLES? Consider planning the party around pickles or fruit spreads, rather than both. Mixing the two can make at-odds odors and a lot more dirty dishes.

CHECK YOUR INVENTORY. You should have enough gear on hand—particularly knives and cutting boards—to accommodate multiple workers. If you're short on stuff, ask guests to bring some . . . especially jars, since they'll be taking those home.

COLLECT YOUR EQUIPMENT. You'll need jars, lids and bands, a magnetic wand, a jar lifter, funnels, a ladle, wooden spoons, plenty of dish towels or paper towels, strainers, cutting boards, knives, a knife sharpener, a vegetable peeler, vitamin C tablets or bottled lemon juice (if preserving cut fruit, like peaches), canning pot(s), and rack(s). An outdoor burner is also helpful.

ASSIGN INGREDIENTS. Unless you have a bumper crop and want to get rid of produce, it's not a bad idea to have everyone bring a portion of the ingredients to share the burden of costs.

COME UP WITH A THEME—BUT TRY NOT TO GO OVERBOARD. Creating a fun atmosphere means pickle making won't overshadow having a good time. However, try not to overdo the theme, since too many canners and cocktails and costumes and party hats may spoil the broth . . . or jam . . . or chutney.

DURING THE CAN JAM: EAT, DRINK, AND BE PREPARED TO TALK CANNING

MONITOR THE WATER. When guests are ready and raring to preserve, waiting around for a giant pot of water to boil can be a major time drain. Time it so the water reaches a full, rolling boil right about the time jars are packed, sealed, and ready to process. It's helpful to keep the pot on low to medium heat and then blast the heat about 20 to 30 minutes before it's time to process. Keep a secondary pot of boiling water (such as a teakettle) on hand in case evaporation in the canning pot becomes an issue.

BRUSH UP. Guests automatically look to you, the host, as the canning leader and may ask you lots of questions. You may ask guests to brush up on the basic canning processes (see page 25, for a refresher) *before* cocktails are poured. If you're new to canning yourself, assign a more seasoned guest to take charge. Either way, it's your job as host to keep the iPod queued, keep drinks refilled, and, most important, assist in making sure jars are packed and processed correctly.

ENCOURAGE HAIR TIES. Hand out rubber bands or bandannas before canning, because there is *nothing* grosser than finding a stray hair in an otherwise perfect jar of pickles. (Trust us. This can happen. We'll spare you the details.)

SERVE A SIGNATURE DRINK. A great drink will jump-start the proceedings. Turn to page 200 for five delicious cocktails that utilize some of Kelly's recipes. These libations will revamp the way guests think about "canned food."

KEEP THE DRINKS FLOWING . . . BUT NOT OVERFLOWING. It's not a bad idea to limit alcohol so guests stay focused on the task at hand. We usually make enough booze available for one or two cocktails per person at the start, then provide another batch of cocktails at the very end. Have plenty of nonalcoholic beverages on hand throughout.

KEEP FOOD SIMPLE . . . BUT YUMMY. Stick with finger food that's good for grazing in between packing jars. Think a vegetable platter, hummus, olives, cheese, fresh bread or crackers, and of course some of your homemade fruit spreads and pickles—a pickle plate! (See Navigating the Pickle Plate, page 196.) The trick is to serve treats that won't spoil if left untouched for an hour or so.

AFTER THE CAN JAM: A SWEET, SAVORY SEND-OFF

HOPE FOR A COMMUNAL CLEANUP. Good guests will stick around until the last pot is washed and put away.

DIVIDE UP THE LOOT. Send everyone home with an equal number of jars.

TAKE A LOAD OFF. After an afternoon of canning, there's nothing better than kicking back with a few party hangers-on—preferably outside under a shady tree—finishing that last cocktail and rewarding yourselves for all your delicious effort.

Caliente in a Can

A spicy, red-hot fiesta

RECIPES: Roasted Tomatillo Salsa Verde (see page 176), Mexican Baby Carrots (see page 122), Carrot Jalapeño Relish (see page 148), Mexi Bell Peppers (see page 147), Carrot Habanero Hot Sauce (see page 150), Fire Salsa Verde (see page 153)

PLAY: Kinky, Mexican Institute of Sound, Nortec Collective, Gipsy Kings, Ojos de Brujo

SIP: Sangria, Mexican beers. For nondrinkers, limeade: Combine the juice of 2 limes in a glass packed with ice and top with seltzer. Stir in a little superfine sugar to taste.

NIBBLE: Empanadas, quesadillas featuring Hot 'n' Spicy Pickled Corn (see page 174), Nachos with Pickled Okra (see page 129), guacamole

CONSIDER: Make latex gloves available to protect guests' hands as they chop and seed hot peppers.

Chutney and Chai

An Indian-inspired curry- and chutney-making soiree

RECIPES: Pear Chili Chutney (see page 179), Green Cherry Tomato Chutney (see page 152), Raisin-Hater's Apple Chutney (see page 181)

PLAY: Classic Bollywood tunes, Bhangra beats, Ravi Shankar, Hare Krishna Kirtan

SIP: For teetotalers, chai tea, Raspberry Rosewater Lassi (see page 103). For drinkers, mango martinis.

NIBBLE: Samosas, pakora, naan bread, mango chunks on skewers dusted with chili powder

CONSIDER: If ethnic cooking isn't your thing, order takeout from an Indian restaurant and serve it on pretty, Indian-inspired plates and platters.

Summertime Jams

Kick off the month of June (which heralds the beginning of canning's busy season) by putting up all sorts of jams made from the season's best berries and fruit.

RECIPES: Strawberry Bay Leaf Jam (see page 72), Strawberry Rhubarb Jam (see page 73), Blueberry Lemon Honey Jam (see page 109), Red Currant Jam (see page 106), Apricot Jam with Honey (see page 96), Blackberry Jam (see page 107)

PLAY: Summertime tunes: "The Tide Is High" by Blondie, "I Gotta Feeling" by the Black Eyed Peas, "Island in the Sun" by Weezer, "Steal My Sunshine" by Len

SIP: Cava, ginger ale garnished with berries, blackberry lemonade, Ginger Key Lime Fizz (see page 202)

NIBBLE: Fun picnic food: mini BLTs, tuna and egg salad sandwiches, and Berries with Cookies and Clotted Cream (see page 113) for dessert

CONSIDER: Cooking sugar can scorch, so assign a canner to frequently stir the pot of jam as it cooks.

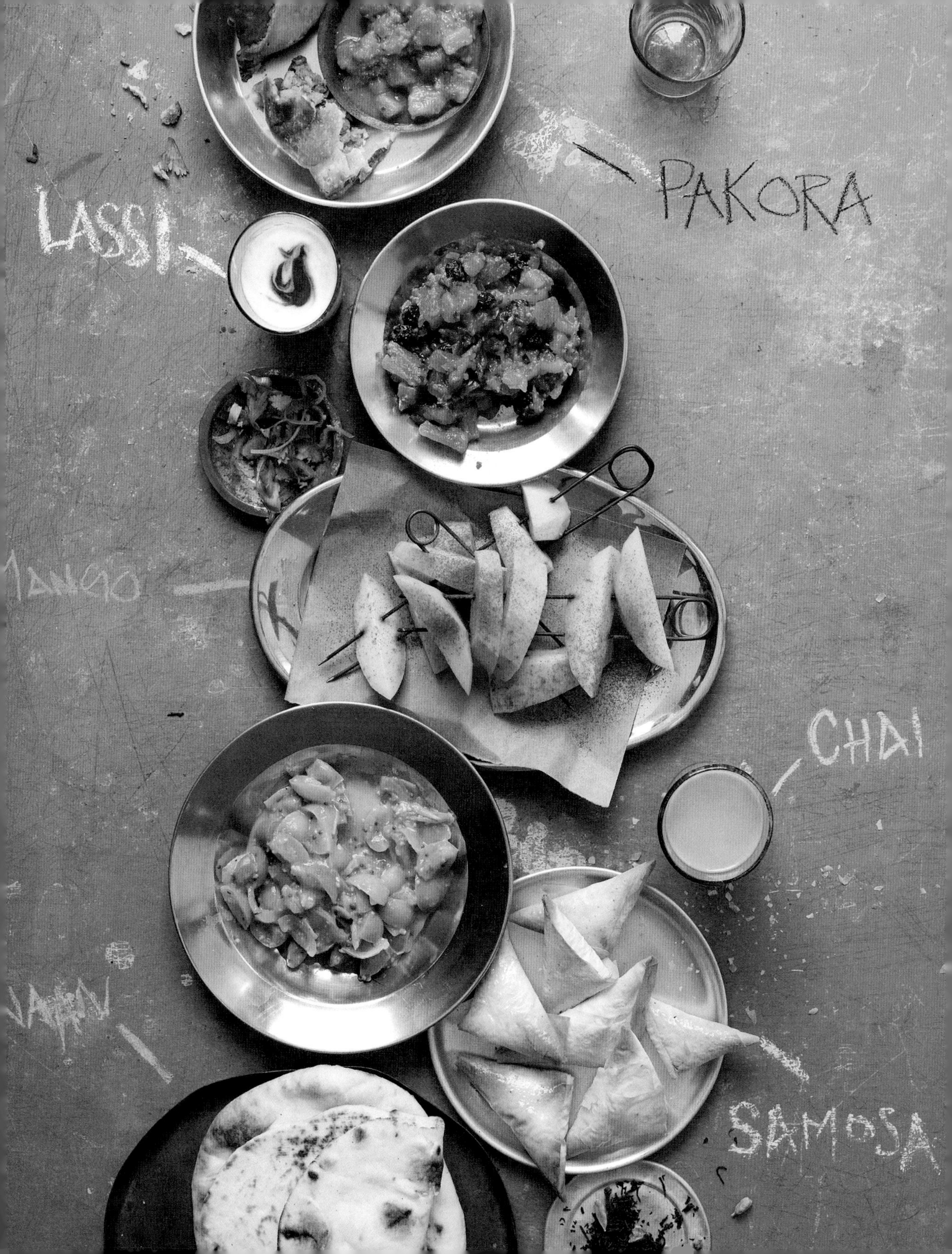
PAKORA
LASSI
CHAI
SAMOSA

Butter and Bourbon

A knee-slapping fruit butter–making hoedown

RECIPES: Apple Maple Butter (see page 158), Pear Butter (see page 162), Mango Chili Butter (see page 100), Banana Butter (see page 160), Banana Vanilla Rum Butter (see page 160), Spiced Pear Cardamom Butter (see page 165)

PLAY: Alt-country, bluegrass, outlaw country like Waylon Jennings, Merle Haggard, Willie Nelson, Johnny Cash, Loretta Lynn, and Dolly Parton

SIP: Bourbon straight, mint julep, Kentucky B&B, bourbon old-fashioned. For teetotalers, try a ginger ale julep: 1 tablespoon crème de menthe syrup stirred into ½ cup ginger ale poured over ice and garnished with fresh mint.

NIBBLE: Pigs in a blanket, Butter-milk Biscuits (see page 162), mini chocolate tarts, Apple Spice Cake (see page 159), walnut bread, candied nuts

CONSIDER: Butters take a little while to cook . . . and a little bourbon goes a long way. So go light on the cocktails . . . unless you want to have a serious hootenanny.

Pregs and Pickled

A pickling shower for the dill-craving mommy-to-be

RECIPES: Pickled Asparagus (see page 77), Wasabi Green Beans (see page 119), Spicy Dill Pickles (see page 142), Chili Pickled Okra (see page 129), Chili Black Pepper Pickled Watermelon (see page 137)

PLAY: Maternal songs ("Little Star" by Madonna, "Sweet Child o' Mine," by Guns N' Roses, "Mamma Mia" by ABBA)

SIP: The guest of honor enjoys a momtini (seltzer cut with red currant syrup or similar in a martini glass), while everybody else sips a Gin Martini with Pickled Ramps (see page 203).

NIBBLE: A pickle plate

CONSIDER: Pickles take at least 2 to 3 weeks to cure after processing, so you won't get to munch what you're making. Have some store-bought artisanal varieties or previous pickles you've canned on hand so Mom can satisfy her salty/sour tooth.

Why Do Moms-to-Be Crave Pickles?

Not all prego ladies crave pickles, of course, but those who do may be mineral deficient due to increased blood volume during pregnancy. This causes existing minerals—particularly sodium—to become diluted, making Mom crave salt. Pregnant women may also experience an increased taste for sour foods, which is the body's way of ensuring they get enough variety in their diet to support weight gain.

NAVIGATING THE PICKLE PLATE

Think of a pickle plate like a cheese platter or even a wine tasting: Go for a selection of light and mild to more puckery and powerful. That way, you never overpower guests' tastebuds with one excessively pungent flavor.

For a well-rounded pickle plate, you might try serving something like mild Pickled Baby Beets with Juniper Berries (see page 76) and Orange Chili Pickled Baby Fennel (see page 173) along with an assortment of medium-sour Dilly Beans (see page 121) and Curry Cauliflower Pickle (see page 125). Then move on to more pungent Spicy Dill Pickles (see page 142), Kimchi (see page 88), Sauerkraut (see page 86), and Southeast Asian Carrot Daikon Pickles (see page 139).

For a more elaborate mix of flavors, include cheeses—again, a range of light to strong—plus breads or crackers, olives, figs, nuts, and of course lots of homemade preserves for spreading—Strawberry Bay Leaf Jam (see page 72), Tarted-Up Grapes (see page 168), Pear Chili Chutney (see page 179). Anne Saxelby, of New York City–based Saxelby Cheesemongers, came up with the following *fromage* accompaniment suggestions for your next pickle plate.

MILD

Pickled Baby Beets with Juniper Berries

PAIR WITH: A bracing blue like gorgonzola (try Bayley Hazen Blue from Jasper Hill Farm, Greensboro, Vermont) or a fresh goat cheese

Orange Chili Pickled Baby Fennel

PAIR WITH: A light and buttery triple crème style (try Saint-André, or Kunik from Nettle Meadow Farm, Warrensburg, New York) or a musky but sweet aged goat cheese (try Gorrotxa from Spain or Manchester from Consider Bardwell Farm, West Pawlet, Vermont)

MILD TO MEDIUM

Curry Cauliflower Pickle

PAIR WITH: A bright and yeasty beer cheese (try Harpersfield washed with Ommegang Abbey Ale from Brovetto Dairy, Jefferson, New York) or a fresh ricotta

Dilly Beans

PAIR WITH: Sharp, biting Cheddars with a touch of Parmesan sweetness (try Cabot Clothbound Cheddar or Cabot Classic Vermont Sharp)

MEDIUM TO SOUR

Spicy Dill Pickles

PAIR WITH: A nutty, buttery cheese with a hint of acidity (try fontina, or Pawlet from Consider Bardwell Farm, Pawlet, Vermont)

Kimchi

PAIR WITH: Something gooey, grassy, and barely pungent (try Reblochon, or Oma from the Von Trapp Farmstead, Mad River Valley, Vermont)

Sauerkraut

PAIR WITH: Aged, nutty, fruity cow's milk cheeses (try Comté, or Pleasant Ridge Reserve from Uplands Cheese Company, Dodgeville, Wisconsin)

15 Tasty Uses for Leftover Pickle Brine

Leftover pickling brine contains some of the produce's nutrients that may have leached out during processing. Brine can also be used to liven up other foods and drinks. Here are 15 ways to make sure that brine doesn't go to waste.

1. Pour it into cocktails. Fruit brine is great with vodka. Vegetable brine is a perfect pairing for gin, vodka, or whiskey and adds a nice kick to Bloody Marys. Or use it in place of salt and lime with a shot of tequila.

2. Combine with hot, just-cooked potatoes for a more pronounced potato salad.

3. When making deviled eggs, stir in a few tablespoons with the yolk mixture.

4. Whisk into salad dressings, from Thousand Island to vinaigrette.

5. Add a splash to simmering water before poaching an egg. The acid helps keep the egg together as it cooks in the saucepan.

6. Stir into soups in need of some extra flavor, from chili to borscht.

7. Mix into ground meat when making hamburger or turkey patties.

8. Use as the "secret ingredient" for outstanding basic beans, from Boston to refried to black.

9. Mix with vegetable juice and drink up.

10. Pour over cubed feta cheese and marinate to create a tangy pickled feta.

11. Pour into ice trays and freeze. Use pickle cubes to keep your Bloody Mary cold.

12. Substitute pickle juice for vinegar in homemade barbecue sauce.

13. Whisk a few drops into eggs for tangy omelets and frittatas.

14. Chop up carrots, cucumbers, cauliflower, onions, cherry tomatoes, whatever veg you have lying around; top with brine and refrigerate.

15. Drink it straight.

Bridal Shower Jam

A lot of crafty, DIY brides like to give away mini jars of preserves at their weddings—why not make a party out of the preparation?

RECIPES: Blackberry Syrup (see page 111), Ginger Key Lime Syrup (see page 62), Raspberry Rosewater Syrup (see page 103), Banana Vanilla Rum Butter (see page 160), Spiced Pear Cardamom Butter (see page 165)

PLAY: "Chapel of Love" by the Dixie Cups, "White Wedding" by Billy Idol, "Single Ladies (Put a Ring On It)" by Beyoncé

SIP: Blackberry Mint Love (see page 203)

NIBBLE: Tea sandwiches filled with cucumbers and dill cream or Pickled Asparagus (see page 77) and Boursin, Brown Sugar Cake with Peach Lavender Jam (see page 99)

CONSIDER: Depending on the size of the event and budget, one 4-ounce jar per guest should do it (see the a handy conversion chart below). Stick to smooth preserves and syrups, because these itty-bitty jars are too small for packing chunkier fruits and vegetables.

NUMBER OF GUESTS	NUMBER OF 4-OUNCE JARS YOU'LL NEED	...WHICH EQUALS THIS IN QUARTS
50	50	7
75	75	10
100	100	13
200	200	26

By all means, get creative with the wedding favor. If you're preserving Blackberry Syrup, for example, attach a pretty tag to each jar that includes a recipe for the cocktail Blackberry Mint Love (see page 203). In the gift bags for members of the wedding party, you might include all the ingredients needed to make the cocktail—mini jars of Blackberry Syrup (see page 111), Mint Simple Syrup (see page 203), a little bottle of vodka, and seltzer plus two fun glasses. After all, there's nothing like an impromptu pre-ceremony cocktail at the hotel to kick-start the festivities!

Raining Tomatoes

When the tomato crop hits in late summer, it hits hard. Gather the troops for some large-scale tomato creations to put up for the winter—you'll be glad you did come January.

RECIPES: Canned Tomatoes (see page 131), Pickled Green Cherry Tomatoes (see page 126), Soy Garlic Cherry Tomatoes (see page 127), Herby Tomatoes (see page 132), Tomato Sauce with Capers and Olives (see page 132), Tomato Ketchup (see page 134), Tangy Orange Tomato Ketchup (see page 136)

PLAY: Canner's choice

SIP: Bloody Mary with Pickled Asparagus (see page 202), ice cold beer, white wine, rosé

NIBBLE: Fresh buffalo mozzarella with basil, olive oil, and salt and pepper for on-the-fly *insalata caprese*

CONSIDER: Make sure to have plenty of bottled lemon juice on hand, since tomatoes must be acidulated to ensure they're safe for long-term storage.

CANNING COCKTAILS

There's more to canning than just jamming and pickling. Canned goods make the freshest and most creative libations. Here are five cocktail creations that can be mixed using your own preserved goodies and a few basic spirits.

Bloody Mary with Pickled Asparagus

¼ cup vodka
1 teaspoon freshly grated horseradish
1 teaspoon Sriracha (Thai hot sauce) or other hot sauce
2 shakes of Worcestershire sauce
A squeeze of lemon juice
Chilled Tomato Puree (see page 132)
Celery salt and pepper to taste
Chilled dark beer (optional)
Pickled Asparagus (see page 77)

Add the vodka, horseradish, hot sauce, Worcestershire, and lemon juice to a pint glass. Top with Tomato Puree. Season with celery salt and pepper. Add beer, if desired, and thoroughly stir. Garnish with a stalk or two of Pickled Asparagus. YIELD: **1 SERVING**

NOTE: This recipe calls for homemade Tomato Puree, but you can use commercial tomato juice as well. I like to rub a mixture of celery salt and sea salt on the rim of the glass and top it off with a splash of dark beer. —Kelly

Kumma Closer

2 Candied Kumquats with Cinnamon and Star Anise plus 1 tablespoon of the syrup (see page 58)
Prosecco

Add the kumquats and syrup to a glass, and top with Prosecco. YIELD: **1 SERVING**

Ginger Key Lime Fizz

¼ cup dark rum, or to taste
¼ cup Ginger Key Lime Syrup (see page 62)
Chilled club soda
Candied ginger
Lime wedge

Add the rum and syrup to a shaker of ice. Gently shake and strain into a glass filled with ice. Top with the soda. Garnish with a small piece of candied ginger and a lime wedge. YIELD: **1 SERVING**

Gin Martini with Pickled Ramps

1 teaspoon dry vermouth (optional)
Gin
1 Pickled Ramp (see page 78)

Swirl the vermouth to coat the inside of a chilled glass; discard the excess. Gently swirl the gin in a shaker of ice and strain into the glass. Garnish with the ramp. Add ice if you like. YIELD: 1 SERVING

Blackberry Mint Love

¼ cup Blackberry Syrup (see page 111)
3 tablespoons Mint Simple Syrup (below)
2–4 tablespoons vodka
Chilled club soda
Sprig of fresh mint

Add the Blackberry Syrup, Mint Simple Syrup, and vodka to a glass filled with ice. Top with the soda and stir. Garnish with the mint sprig. YIELD: 1 SERVING

Mint Simple Syrup

1¼ cups packed fresh mint leaves, chopped
1 cup sugar
1 cup water

Bring the mint, sugar, and water to a boil in a small saucepan, stirring to dissolve the sugar. Reduce the heat to a simmer and cook for 3 minutes. Strain into a heatproof container, pressing down on the mint to extract as much minty juice as possible. Cover and chill completely. Keeps for 2 weeks. YIELD: 1½ CUPS

Jar Decor

If you want to give away some of your canned goods as gifts, it's a nice touch to gussy up the jars. Pretty tags, ribbon, raffia, and decorative fabric or paper jar toppers add a rustic touch.

A word of warning: When it comes to jar attire, less is definitely more. Stick with a pretty tag or sticker, some ribbon or raffia ties, *or* a fabric jar topper. Too much adornment of your beautiful jars can quickly start to resemble a child's craft project gone awry. Some simple and chic suggestions:

FABRIC TOPPERS

Use a pair of scissors—either straight edged or decorative edged—to cut a circle of simple fabric ½ to 1 inch larger than the jar lid. If you want, select fabric colors that correspond with the season—bright colors for summer, pastels for spring—or that contrast with the color of the preserves. Secure underneath the screw band and tie with a strip of raffia, string, or ribbon. For a more minimalist look, use a scrap of parchment paper cut the same way; secure with a white rubber band and adorn with a metal-rimmed hang tag.

PAPER TOPPERS

Using pretty wrapping paper (this is a great use for scraps that are too small to use for other wrapping), scrapbook paper, or even a picture from a magazine, cut a circle the size of the lid and adhere to the lid with a drop of glue. Secure with a screw band.

TRIM

Ribbon, colored string, thin elastic cord, raffia, twine, even rickrack can look nice.

LABELS

Here's where you can tap into your inner crafter without looking like you went craft crazy. Consider hanging a label—metal rimmed, plain paper, cardboard—from a bit of ribbon, colored string, or raffia. Or label the jar directly. Don't forget to date it as well. A few ideas:

WRITE IT. Adhere a plain white printing label directly to a jar with the date and contents written in a vintage typewriter font . . . or whatever font catches your eye.

STAMP IT. Fasten a metal-rimmed circular tag stamped with a symbol that reflects the jar's contents to a strip of raffia and tie to the jar. For example, you might use a bee stamp on the label of a jar of Grapefruit Honey Jam. Include a second, larger cardboard hanging tag for added dimension.

PAINT IT. Swiping a bit of paint on an oversize label, then writing the jar's contents over it is a sneaky way to come across as effortlessly artistic.

INCLUDE A RECIPE. Label and date the contents on one side of a large paper label. On the other side, include a recipe or suggestion for how to use the food (a recipe for Buttermilk Biscuits on the back of a Pear Butter label, for example).

SAVE PAPER. Use glass-safe paint pens to label the jar itself. Make sure the color you use shows up against the contents of the glass. Painted jars should not be used again for canning.

Canning
Conundrums

If you follow the directions in the book and make a point of working with fresh, clean produce and clean equipment,

you really shouldn't have a problem when canning—it's almost surprising how rarely mishaps occur.

Nevertheless, snafus will occur every now and again that may make you wonder what the heck went wrong and whether your canned food is safe to eat. In most instances, it is. But learning the cause of the problem will help you prevent it from happening again and keep you from having to ask yourself the question in the first place. Here are some of the more common canning problems we've seen, their causes, and some hindsight to prevent their recurrence.

General Canning Concerns

"My jar didn't seal."

Not a big problem. Either refrigerate the item and treat it like any other perishable or reprocess it following the instructions given in the recipe. Some reasons for seal failure:

- You may have left too much headspace in the jar. Leaving too much can prevent a vacuum from forming, so always stick to the amount indicated in the recipe.

- You may have forgotten to check for air bubbles. Tapping the bottom of the packed jar against the counter or running a butter knife through the mixture before sealing should release trapped air bubbles.

- You may have underprocessed the item or forgotten to adjust for altitude. Starting the clock for processing *after* the canning pot loaded with jars comes to a full, rolling boil should prevent this. Take a few minutes to find out your elevation and tweak processing times accordingly.

- The canning jar itself may have been nicked or scratched, or the gasket on the lid may have been dented. Or food particles got trapped around the lid. All of this opens the door to air and bacteria, which prevents a seal. Always wipe down jar rims before sealing.

- There was not enough water covering the jars during processing. Make sure jars are submerged by at least 2 inches of water to ensure a tight seal. Keep a secondary pot of boiling water on hand should evaporation in the canning pot become an issue during processing.

"My jar sealed—then unsealed. What happened?"

Dump this jar. While it's probably the result of something relatively innocuous like underprocessing or too much headspace, air bubbles, or gunk around the rim of the jar, there is a chance there wasn't enough acid in the item to ensure a long-term seal (a salsa of your own creation, let's say, that combined more low-acid veggies than the recipe called for, or a pickle recipe diluted with too much water). Try to follow precise measurements, particularly in recipes that call for low-acid (any vegetable) ingredients, since dangerous bacteria can grow in low-acid environments.

"The canning liquid is below the top of the food."

- You may have forgotten to check for air bubbles.

- The food may have been packed too tightly. If the food looks bruised or crushed, it was packed too tightly.

- The food was packed raw. Sometimes it's preferable to use the hot pack method . . . especially when canning whole fruits and vegetables.

- The screw band was too loose, allowing juice to escape during processing.

- Starchy food like corn absorbed liquid.

As long as the jar is sealed, some liquid loss is perfectly safe. If, however, *half* the liquid is gone, don't store it in the larder—treat it like a perishable; refrigerate the jar and eat the contents within 2 or 3 days.

"The food is dark at the top of the jar."

- The food wasn't fully submerged in canning liquid, so it oxidized in the presence of air. In most cases, it is still safe to eat.

- Food like peeled peaches, apples, or nectarines wasn't treated in an anti-browning solution.

- There was too much air in the jar due to improper headspace or air bubble removal.

"The food is a weird color."

- Some foods, such as asparagus, brussels sprouts, corn, garlic, and pears, can change colors when processed, but they're still perfectly safe to eat. But if foods turn black, brown, or gray, it means either there were too many minerals in the water or a reactive metal—brass, zinc, aluminum, iron, copper—was used during the cooking phase. To prevent this, use soft water and can only with stainless steel and heat-resistant nonmetallic utensils.

"The inside of my pot looks filmy. And my jars look cloudy."

- There's probably a buildup of hard water in your pot and jars. Soak for an hour or so in a solution containing 1 cup vinegar to 1 gallon water.

"How come the underside of the lid is dark?"

- The lid came into contact with reactive metal. Use only nonmetallic utensils when handling lids. The food is still safe to eat.

"How come the lid is buckled?"

- This may mean the food has spoiled. Give it a smell to confirm. If it smells "off," toss it.

- It could mean the lid was too tight. Screw bands should be fingertip tight, not *vise* tight.

"The food has mold growing on top."

- You may have forgotten to check for air bubbles.

- You may have left insufficient headspace.

- You may have underprocessed it.

In all instances, don't scrape off the mold and think the product is safe. Mold growth can raise the pH of the food, making high-acid jams become low-acid breeding grounds for botulism or other bacterial spoilage. Toss it.

Fruit Spread Snafus

"My jam didn't set."

- You may not have used enough sugar or pectin. Sometimes though not always this can be remedied by adding more pectin to the spread as it cooks, which is why it's good to keep a couple of packs of commercial pectin on hand just in case.

- You may have used overripe fruit. Older fruit may not contain enough acid to ensure a gel.

- You may have cooked the recipe too long. Fruit spreads are generally very forgiving, but cooking a spread too long could cause pectin to break down, leaving you with a watery spread.

"My jam looks suspiciously dark."

- You may have stored it in too light or too warm a location. Try to store preserves in a dark place in the 70°F range.

- You may have overcooked it. Adhere to the cooking times in your recipe.

"Why are crystals in my fruit spread?"

- You may not have stirred enough to allow sugar to completely dissolve during cooking. You can never stir too much when making spreads (this includes ketchups)!

Pickle Problems

"My pickles aren't crisp."

- It may mean too little salt was used or the vinegar was less than 5 percent acidity. Use only vinegars that say "5 percent acidity" on the bottles.

- You may have forgotten to discard the blossom end on cucumbers. The blossoms may contain an enzyme that hastens softening.

- You may have overcooked the produce or overprocessed the jars.

"My pickles are shriveled."

- It may mean they were heat processed too long or too much salt, sugar, or vinegar was used.

"My pickles are hollow."

- It means the produce was overripe at the time of canning. A good way to check: If a cucumber sinks in a bowl of water, it's ripe for canning. If it floats, it contains too much air and should just be eaten fresh.

"My pickles are dark."

- It may mean table salt was used in the brine. Use only kosher or canning salt.

- It may be the result of hard water. Use soft water instead.

- It may mean reactive pots and utensils were used. Use nonreactive stainless steel pots and nonmetal utensils.

- It may be that the spices in the jar—curry, turmeric—turned the pickles a dark color.

"My pickle brine is cloudy."

- It may be a sign of spoilage. Give it a smell to confirm. If it's "off," toss it.

- It may mean table salt was used. Use only kosher or canning salt.

- It could mean there was too much starch in vegetables like corn. Don't use overmature starchy produce.

- It could be a sign of hard water. Use soft water instead.

Fermentation Kerfuffles

"My fermented food is slippery and mushy."

- This usually means too little salt was used and bad bacteria have taken hold. If this is accompanied by a not-so-nice smell, dump it.

"There's white sediment in my fermented pickles."

- It means the naturally occurring yeast and bacteria that feed on the brine weren't regularly skimmed off. Yeast should be skimmed every day. But the product should otherwise be safe.

- It may mean table salt was used in the brine. Use only kosher or canning salt.

"There's white scum growing on my sauerkraut."

- This is totally normal. It means the kraut is fermenting properly. Remember to skim off the scum every day.

"My sauerkraut/kimchi has changed color."

- It may be because ground spices were used, which caused the brine to change color. This is perfectly safe, but you can always use whole spices instead.

- It may be the result of minerals in hard water. Use soft water instead.

- It may mean the kraut vessel used was reactive. Use food-grade plastic, enamelware, glass, stainless steel, or ceramic instead.

"My sauerkraut/kimchi is moldy."

- It may mean the fermentation temperature was too high—anything over 75° to 80°F.

- It may mean the food wasn't fully submerged in brine.

  In either case, dump it.

Acknowledgments

We have a lot of people we'd like to thank for this book.

First and foremost, we'd like to thank our editor, Julie Will, at Rodale for her unflagging support, knowledge, and intuition, plus her willingness to schlep out to Bed Stuy—and for having a special weakness for Kelly's blueberry lemongrass syrup. Thank you, Julie, you're a real pleasure to work with.

Thanks to Jen King and Claire Jeffers (and Tom Petty) for their hard work testing and tasting these recipes. We really could not have finished this project without you gals!

And thanks to our agent, Maura Kye-Casella, for being as much of a friend as business associate. You helped shape this project before the first word was written or the first pickle brined.

Many people at Rodale contributed to the look of this book, notably Amy King, Kara Plikaitis, and Nancy N. Bailey. Ellen Silverman, working with stylists Christine Rudolph and Adrienne Anderson, created gorgeous, mouthwatering photographs of recipes using canned food that looks nothing like "canned food." Ladies, you are the very best at what you do, and we wish we could work with you all the time.

Finally, thanks to all the family members, friends, and peers who endlessly tasted and listened to us talk about canning: Jake Wilson, Peter Agoston, Kai Hill, Barb Price, Gale Wilson, Paula Szuchman, Shawna DeWitt, Annaliese Griffin, Ellen Watkins, Yvonne Hyde, Sam and Sandra Watkins, Anne Saxelby, Michael Kokas and Jan Greer, Tracy West, Charlie and Suzanne Luker, Bob McClure, Katy Anders, Chin Velasquez, Kathryn Young, Susan Guida, and Brendan Perry. A special thank-you to Kelly's folks, Dick and Gail Geary, for their unwavering support and encouragement (thanks, Dad, for the "Let's Get Pickled" title idea, sorry it didn't work out). And to Kelly's wonderful doggers, Murray (R.I.P.) and Pickles, for waiting long hours with their tiny legs crossed for her to come home!

Index

Underscored page references indicate boxed text. **Boldfaced** page references indicate photographs.